story
PRIORITY

A **FRESH EXPRESSIONS** BOOK

story PRIORITY

**How to Change Lives
Using the 468 Jesus
Narratives**

Verlon Fosner

invite
PRESS

Plano, Texas

Story Priority
How to Change Lives Using the 468 Jesus Narratives

Copyright © 2024 by Verlon Fosner

This book is printed on acid-free, elemental chlorine-free paper.

ISBN: Paperback: 9781963265217; eBook 9781963265224

24 25 26 27 28 29 30 31 32 33 —10 9 8 7 6 5 4 3 2 1

MANUFACTURED in the UNITED STATES of AMERICA

To the elders, deacons, pastors, and staff
who fearlessly sailed with me into the fog
to land upon the shores of the historic kerygma.
Together we rediscovered the Jesus Stories
and found them to be more authoritative
and powerful than we could have imagined—
such that we rebuilt our very faith and ministries
and church upon them.
Bless you all!

Contents

INTRODUCTION   xi

CHAPTER ONE
My Words—Build Your Life on Them   1

CHAPTER TWO
Remember Me—and Bring Back the Table   13

CHAPTER THREE
Offer My Favor—to the Poor, the Blind, the Oppressed   27

CHAPTER FOUR
Be Witnesses to Me—Tell My Stories   39

CHAPTER FIVE
Go Preach the Gospel—the Way I Did   55

CHAPTER SIX
Make Disciples—Teach Them What I Told You   75

CHAPTER SEVEN
Build My Church—by Listening to Me   89

CONCLUSION   111

APPENDIX A
What the First Church Proclaimed   115

APPENDIX B
A Guide to Telling Jesus Stories   123

APPENDIX C
468 Stories from the Life of Christ   125

Introduction

I am sixty-four years old and still remember the flannel graph lessons in my Sunday school class as a child. For those who have never sat through a flannel graph teaching, they consisted of paper cut-outs of Bible characters and scenes that the teacher would stick onto a three-by-four-foot flannel board while telling a Bible story. They were old school but sure were impactful. To this day I remember the ink smell as the teacher pulled the cut-outs from a large white envelope. She would then read from a curriculum book she held in one hand while placing the colorful images on the flannel board with the other. The stories would develop one figure after another until twelve to fifteen vivid pictures filled the board. I don't remember if my teachers were particularly compelling as orators, but I do remember those stories. The backdrops, the landscapes, the animals, and the expressions on the characters' faces created a deep feeling in me. My young faith was built upon those pictured stories.

Sadly, I have very few memories of Jesus Stories after I graduated from those children's classes. Although I was a pastor's son and attended church four times a week, the spiritual content seemed to shift from stories to outlines and scriptural principles once I got into junior high and beyond. I interpreted this to mean that Jesus Stories were the elementary material of the Bible, but now I had matriculated on to deeper teachings.

When I enrolled in preaching classes as an undergrad in a theology program, we were taught to form our sermons and teachings based on principles of interpretation using hermeneutics, exegesis, contextualization, and tracking the etymology of scriptural words, all set upon the unquestioned foundation of systematic theology. So, when I began ministry as a youth pastor, I did what I was taught: I prepared teachings around scriptural reasonings, although they were attuned to youth issues. But the Jesus Stories were largely absent in those youth lessons.

Later, when I was called to minister to adults, my teaching and systematic reasonings deepened significantly. In fact, I was rewarded every time I took adult crowds into "new depths" of scripture; my teaching content was now something very different than the Jesus Stories that shaped my faith as a child. But of course, that was the expectation; that was what I was trained to do. This understanding of teaching would guide me unabated for the first twenty-seven years of ministry. And yet, as I sit here typing these words today, I only vaguely recall any of my teaching outlines through the years. But I sure remember the lessons from that children's classroom in Klamath Falls, Oregon. We sat spellbound as those stories unfolded before us.

Now, I am not proposing a return to the flannel graph era, but I am proposing a return to the Jesus Stories, even for adults. However, I do suggest several reasons for realigning ourselves with the primary speaking content that was used during the Apostolic era. While they did not have the full canon as we do today, they did have the vibrant life and stories of Jesus, which they retold over and over again. Young John Mark was the first to have the idea of writing these stories down so that other Christ-followers could retell them everywhere they went. These Jesus Stories were different from anything that had appeared in the world of literature prior.[1] Focusing on the Jesus Stories, such as they did, created a different tone of the gospel than what is commonly practiced today. Author Alan Hirsch writes, "Reading the Gospels through the Epistles creates a disturbing distortion. The Gospels are not taken seriously as prescriptive texts for life, mission, and discipleship."[2]

There are significant differences between the church of this Reformation era (1517 AD–present) and the church of the Apostolic era (33 AD–320 AD). For all our theological reflections, we are collectively numb to the early Christian approaches. Modernism has placed a pair of glasses on us that has colored our reading of the New Testament. Theologian and author Alan Streett states that it is difficult for twenty-first-century Christians to visualize a Christian banquet version of the church.[3] This blindness not only affects our reading of the ecclesial patterns of the first church, but also how those in the early church preached. In the wake of the modernist era many leaders hold the gospel stories as *elemental*, while holding other portions of scripture as *deeper teachings*. This attitude needs to be reversed. I love the words of Paul: "I am not ashamed of the Gospel of Christ, for it is the power of God to salvation for everyone who believes, for the Jew and for the Greek" (Rom. 1:16). Paul and crew were deeply impressed by the gospel stories because of the divine power— the power to draw people to salvation—that was released when they told them.

With today's church becoming so ingrown and disconnected from secular society, we need a serious review of the spiritual con-

---

1. Michael Green, *Evangelism in the Early Church* (Grand Rapids, MI: Eerdmans, 2003), 347.

2. Alan Hirsch and Michael Frost, *The Shaping of Things to Come: Innovation and Mission for the 21st Century* (Grand Rapids, MI: Baker Books, 2003), 113.

3. Alan Streett, *Subversive Meals: An Analysis of the Lord's Supper under Roman Domination during the First Century* (Eugene, OR: Pickwick, 2013), 287.

tent we are using. In such a review, one cannot help but acknowledge that the first apostles relied on different spiritual content than we practice. They were laser focused on the life and stories of Jesus. To our credit, we have grabbed the grand purposes of Jesus' life in our teachings, but the first followers grabbed the details from each story of his life. The minutiae of his life talked louder to them than it does to us. The Jesus Stories consumed them and flowed into their conversations, preaching, evangelism, and discipleship.

In 2007 our historic church in Seattle felt directed by the Spirit to open dinner churches throughout the city.[4] These dinners were modeled after the New Passover Jesus tables used by the early church throughout the first 300 years of Christianity. Very quickly these dinner rooms started to fill up with secular people. It was remarkable. Soon we were spreading these Jesus tables from one neighborhood to the next and were engaging with a multitude of unreached neighbors most evenings of the week. From that tableside vantage point, we observed the surprising power of the Jesus Stories to capture the imagination of secular people and draw them toward Christ. Realizing we were not engaged in an innovation but rather in a recovery project, we started focusing our spiritual content on the Jesus Stories like the apostles of the first church. We learned very quickly that secular, agnostic, and even atheistic people enjoyed talking about the life of Christ. It wasn't pure Christianity that bothered them, it was Churchianity—at least our version of it.

---

4.   In 2007 Westminster Community Church started planting historic dinner churches throughout the city of Seattle. By partnering with multiple congregations in the city, they have now opened up fifteen Jesus Tables in Seattle proper, with an average attendance of seventy-five people.

A large opportunity now exists for the church if we can re-grip the gospel and the Jesus Stories like the first church held them. For any group that chooses to prioritize the Jesus Stories, many things will be reframed: their understanding of spiritual formation, evangelism, discipleship, preaching, leadership, and even the ministry of reconciliation. For these reasons and more, I propose a return to the stories from the life of Christ. What follows are theological reflections that teach us to prioritize the 468 Jesus Stories.

My Words—Build Your Life on Them

J esus instructed his disciples to prioritize his words and stories, which they did. They told and retold the Jesus Stories because they were enraptured by his every word and deed. Matthew 7:24ff captures this truth with the story of two builders: one who builds their house on sand, and another who builds their house on rock. When floods and winds came the house on sand experienced a thorough and complete collapse, while the house on rock stood firm. Jesus interpreted this story to mean that everyone who builds their life on "his words" are the ones building on rock, but everyone who ignores "his words" and builds their lives upon other teaching materials will experience a great crash in times of testing.

It is popular in Christian circles today to shuffle the gospel content together with the rest of scripture without discerning the difference between the two. As much as I love reading the Old Testament stories, pouring through the Psalms and Isaiah to massage my tired soul, as well as reading Paul's letters, we must learn to honor the preeminence of Jesus' content. Because according to our Lord, the only spiritual materials available on this earth stalwart enough to withstand all the storms that might bluster against us are "his words."

Repositioning Our Faith

Most Christians today have built their faith on all things scriptural. How different is that from the first Christians who built their faith on all things Jesus Stories? I could prove this from many angles, but for now let's consider the oft-repeated scriptural phrase "Christ the Cornerstone" to observe how the first church constructed their faith:

> Jesus is "the stone the builders rejected, which has become the cornerstone." (Acts 4:11)

> We are "members of his household, built on the foundation of the apostles with Christ Jesus himself as the chief cornerstone". (Eph. 2:19–20)

> You are coming to Christ, who is the living cornerstone of God's temple. (1 Pet. 2:4 NLT)

Jesus as our cornerstone is more than a theological notion. The early Christians talked about Jesus as their cornerstone because Jesus was all they talked about. Every time they gathered, they remembered him, retold his stories, re-spoke his words. Their faith was not only built on Jesus as a matter of theology but of practicality. So when they spoke of the faith that dwelt within them, it was the Jesus Stories that came out. I wonder how different our Christianity would be if we remained focused on the stories and words of Jesus like they did. Shifting the practical cornerstone from Jesus Stories to Bible studies has had a greater impact on the church than most realize.

To be fair, an accurate understanding of the life of Jesus requires the Judaic history as is revealed in the Old Testament and provides a rich backdrop for the gospel narratives. This is one of many reasons to honor the full canon and study the full scriptures. However, I still argue for allowing the Jesus Stories to serve as the primary foundation of our faith. There is a reason why our secular neighbors are not interested in talking with us about spirituality. Our words have become too infused with teaching phrases and bullet points. Truthfully, most of us sense this. We know that we cannot repeat what we heard from the pulpit on Sunday at our workplace. When we repeat Bible teaching our secular friends will sit back, but when we tell Jesus Stories they will lean forward.

That is exactly what repositioning our faith on the Jesus Stories does. Peter spoke to this in 1 Peter 3:15, about always being ready to give an answer for the hope that resides within us. Imagine how much easier that was during the Apostolic era when explanations of faith were based solely on the Jesus Stories. Contrast that with the challenge we now have when our explanations of faith are based on the full canon and its interpretative complexities. While we have been enriched by the fullness of scripture, it hasn't made it easy for us to be instantly ready to explain our faith to a secular friend. But repositioning our faith to be based on the Jesus Stories makes spiritual conversations a matter of storytelling rather than a matter of apologetics. I'm not suggesting you do a hostile takeover of the conversation in your lunchroom; there is a Spirit-led timing involved. However, when a conversation with a secular friend naturally turns spiritual, it is wonderful to have Jesus Stories start bubbling up. To have poured ourselves into the Jesus Stories for our own faith naturally readies us to inspire faith in others by those same stories.

A Unified Canon

Now, don't get me wrong—I am not devaluing the Holy Bible as much as it might appear. I believe in the inspired scriptures and recognize they are useful for teaching, correcting, and training in righteousness (2 Tim. 3:16). However, when the third-century church adopted the sixty-six books of the canon, they formalized a commingled milieu of writings that created a very different spiritual content than what had been used by the apostles. With the full scriptures came great blessing, but there also came an unintended consequence: the Jesus Stories lost their primacy. We must recognize the difference this made. It is the equivalent of adding beef, vegetables, and potatoes to a tomato base. What was tomato soup has now become stew. While both might be good, they are certainly different. Similarly, the specialness and singularity of the life and times of Jesus was diluted. We need to win back the centrality of Jesus Stories.

Topography of Scripture

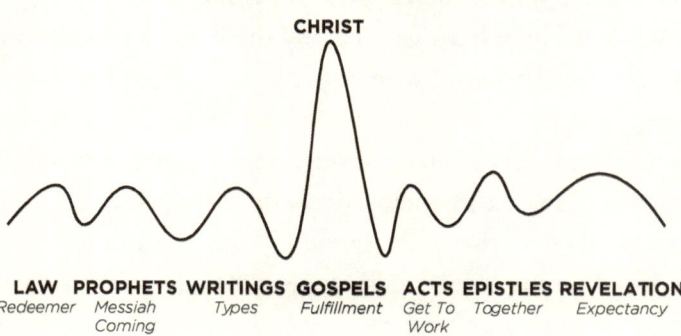

While all scripture is needful, not all scripture is equal. Theology Professor David Olson likened the unity of the scriptures to a topographical map in which the Law, the Prophets, and the Writings were written in anticipation of the coming Messiah. Similarly, Acts, the Epistles, and Revelation were written as a reflection of the life of Jesus. Thus, the majority of Scripture exists in the shadow of the Gospels—the Living Word, the Life of Jesus. Treating all scripture as equal, when they were not written that way, has misshaped us over the centuries.

There is great value in recovering the primacy and superiority of Jesus' words and stories for the church. Present-day evangelical theology tends to come from the Epistles, but it needs to come from the Gospels.[1] However, when the church concentrates on the life of Jesus, a fuller disclosure of the partnership between God and man is revealed.[2] There is something significant to be recaptured here.

The Story Difference

Jesus used stories like no teacher before him. We need to stop for a moment and realize that our Master chose story-form communication for a reason. What is that reason? When Jesus told his stories, even the sinners listened. This is an important consideration in post-Christian America. Jesus Stories can do something in the non-churched community that teaching outlines cannot; they can speak to the secular-formed heart. According to theologian and author Leonard Sweet, the human brain processes forty thoughts per second while listening to a story.[3] Teaching outlines, on the other hand, are progressive and sequential, and lead the listener down a narrow path to a particular conclusion. While many Christians flourish with this guided-thought form of teaching, secular people often find it coercive and controlling. They react to our guided speaking form even before they react to our

---

1. David Olson, presentation at the New Conspirators Conference, Bethany Community Church, Seattle, WA, February 2008.

2. Harvey Cox, *The Secular City: A Celebration of Its Liberties and an Invitation to Its Discipline* (New York: Macmillan, 1965), 112.

3. Leonard Sweet, *From Tablet to Table: Where Community Is Found and Identity Is Formed* (Colorado Springs: NavPress, 2014), 30.

Christian truths. You might like peaches, but if someone insisted on standing you against a barn and throwing peaches at your face for you to bite out of the air, you might not like peaches anymore. This is what much of our teaching feels like to secular people and makes them reject the Christian message before they even taste it. However, Jesus Stories do not force people to a predefined conclusion; they allow people to wander around that story making connections with the great questions and needs of their hearts. Are we willing to use the story-form Gospel?

Their One and Only Message

Reading, interpreting, and teaching biblical scripture has become the primary spiritual task of our day. And we are good at it. With practiced hermeneutics, exegesis, etymology-based word studies, and sequential systematic theology, we have developed a form of spiritual content that is outlined, bullet-pointed, and mechanical. Of course, that makes sense for this scientific, rational, and modernist era!

The first church, however, held a gospel that was narrative and relational, and flowed from a particular life—Jesus' life. His goings and comings and stories became the speaking content for the first three centuries. While their recitations and interactions with the Jesus Stories were simple, they stirred the human soul to its depths. Christian author Rex Miller states that the reason Jesus' words were so powerful was because they contained the living essence of Jesus' presence.[4] The first church understood that to share the Jesus Stories was to pour the very person of Jesus right into the listeners' hearts.

---

4.   Rex M. Miller, *The Millennium Matrix* (San Francisco: Jossey-Bass, 2004), 24.

The church's differing eras have relied on different transformative agents. The Reformation era that we live in has relied heavily on the Holy Bible as our foundation for the faith. The Christendom era relied on cathedrals, candles, stained-glassed images, and icons to be transformative features. But the Apostolic era relied on the life of Jesus. Jesus and his stories were the cornerstone of this era's preaching and Christian formation. A New Testament search of the key words *preach, teach, proclaim,* and *testify* reveals ninety-four usages that clearly identify Jesus and his stories as their speaking subject.[5] (See appendix A.) In fact, only ten times are those key words used without a stated association with the Jesus narratives.

In my view it is not possible to draw any other conclusion than that the spiritual content of the first church was monopolized by recitations, reflections, and references to the life and stories of Jesus. Oxford professor emeritus Michael Green reports, "The early preachers of the good news had one subject and one only. Jesus. This was their word, which they broadcast so assiduously."[6] May Jesus help us become equally enthralled with his 468 stories.

The Different Protestant Message

Five hundred years ago the Church recrafted its gatherings, preaching, and discipleship. The way the new Protestant church began functioning had never been done before. It did not come from scripture anywhere. This version of church was developed by Luther, Calvin, Zwingli, Arminius, and others, most of whom were theology professors, so the classroom setting, which was

5. Search was performed in the New International Version (NIV).
6. Green, *Evangelism in the Early Church*, 80.

natural to them, became the form of church for the many congregants who broke away from Catholicism.

The reformers seemingly felt a need for something that looked different from the sacred-space cathedrals. In these teaching-based environments, everyone sat in rows facing forward and listened to teachings from the word of God in a one-way discourse, similar to the lecturing professors. The obvious need was to teach the new congregants who had left Catholicism how to become the priest of their own home. These factors, commingled with the Gutenberg Press printing copies of the Bible for everyone, made it possible for each attendee to open their Bible and be taught by a pastor on a stage and podium to interpret the scriptures. This has remained the basic structure of Christian gathering for the past 500 years.

Also, at the time of the Reformation, Europe was completely Christianized, so almost everyone attended church.[7] The only question was, Catholic or Protestant church? Anyone walking into any church had a foundational knowledge of the tenets of Christianity. For pastors to assume that level of knowledge and draw people into scriptural teaching outlines was appropriate. In fact, teaching-based approaches have worked well through the centuries, so long as there was a preponderance of people holding to a Judeo worldview. But in the mid-1900s, a secular worldview became more prominent, and teaching-based approaches began to lose traction. Many denominations slipped into decline. Today, with the majority of the West holding a secular worldview, reevaluating our Bible teaching–centric gatherings might be in order.

7. Jim Heugel, "The Reformation," Lecture, Northwest University, Kirkland, WA, February 15, 2011.

The Great Christian Adventure

Today we live on the waning edge of the Reformation era. And true to our history, most Christian leaders still feel assigned to teach scripture more than reveal the Jesus Stories. Even when they speak of the gospel, they talk more *about* Jesus than the details of his life and words and stories like the first church did. Similarly, most Christ-followers hold to the *story* of Jesus without delving into the *stories* of Jesus. To believe the gospel, but not immerse ourselves in Jesus' life and words and narratives, creates a weakness in our faith and effectiveness in mission. But returning to the manner of the first church and pouring ourselves into those vibrant stories will cause something new to arise within us. These stories will not only rebuild a robust foundation under our faith, but they will also empower us for advancing Jesus' kingdom in very unexpected ways. In short, reprioritizing the Jesus Stories will sign us up for the great Christian adventure we were expecting when we first said yes.

Practical Approaches

Anyone desiring to reposition their faith on the Jesus Stories would do well to start reading and meditating on the Gospel stories as their daily devotional approach. But rather than reading through these stories as though they are the junior varsity materials of the Bible, start reading through them as though you expect Jesus to talk to you in a very deep way. Suddenly, they will come alive in a new way. The Gospels are the varsity materials of the scriptures.

My approach to enriching my faith is to read and meditate on two or three Jesus Stories every week. Here are some approaches:

- Right now, early in the mornings and with coffee in hand, I am working my way slowly through the book of Mark. It has taken me several months to get through chapter 7 alone. Notably, most of my preaching and teaching have flowed directly from my morning Jesus Story reflections. Sometimes I read these stories to my wife Melodee, and our insights always deepen as we talk.

- Order a copy of the Jesus Stories Bible, which was released by the American Bible Society in 2021. It is a Contemporary English Version (CEV) printing of the Gospels and Acts that has removed the verse numbers, which enables fluidity from story to story. You can order a copy at www.DinnerChurch.Com/Resources.

- Appendix C of this book has listed the Jesus Story titles, which may be helpful for finding stories that address certain challenges you are facing.

One particular student in our Dinner Church School of Leadership graduate program decided to delve into the Jesus Stories as his devotional approach. He reported back after some months that the stories came alive in him like he'd never experienced before. Soon they were drifting into his conversations, teachings, and preaching. People started commenting to him about the extra measure of strength they sensed, and when he told them that the Jesus Stories were prompting a new anointing, they started reading the Gospels in a fresh way as well. A noticeable change in their faith began to occur in all of them.

Do you have a Bible? Does that Bible have the Gospels included? Then you have what it takes to start repositioning your faith on Jesus' words, works, and stories. But hold on, because things are about to get adventuresome in your Christian experience.

Remember Me—and Bring Back the Table

A significant gospel narrative that directs us to prioritize Jesus' stories was when he uttered that famous phrase, "Remember me." But we must first set the backdrop of the Last Supper. When Jesus was on earth, he followed a pattern of healing by day and having dinner with sinners by night. This strategy has gone largely unnoticed by the church, but if you read back through the gospels with that two-part schedule in mind, you'll see it. Christian historian J. Dominic Crossan stated that to watch a day in the life of Jesus is to see him healing and eating, and that these were the twin pillars of the Jesus tradition.[1] Most leaders readily see healing throughout scripture but are surprised at the suggestion that eating was one of Jesus' intentional strategies.

The New Passover

Jesus' consistent use of the table forged a vision for Christian gatherings. However, the Last Supper became the deepest instruction, because it was there Jesus gave verbal instructions to his disciples. All four Gospels agree that Jesus traveled to Jerusalem to celebrate

---

1. Graydon Snyder, Julian Hills, and Richard Gardner, *Common Life in the Early Church* (Harrisburg, PA: Trinity Press International, 1998), 141.

the Passover week and that he died on Friday. It is therefore no surprise that the synoptic Gospels characterize Jesus' final meal as a Passover supper.[2] However, at this final Passover, Jesus intentionally altered the historic readings with its rich "rescue remembrance" meaning and left the disciples with a refreshed pattern for meeting together. This was to include (1) gathering the isolated, (2) eating together, and (3) talking about him. A growing number of scholars now refer to this pivot as the New Passover, which is a rich vision for the church. Leonard Sweet states, "When Jesus was saying 'Do this in remembrance of me,' he was saying 'Do table in remembrance of me.'"[3] From Acts 2 forward it is obvious the disciples took this directive seriously, and they started gathering liminal people to their tables, eating together, and talking about Jesus.

While this pattern is visible throughout the New Testament, it is wonderfully clear in Corinth almost thirty years after the Resurrection. First Corinthians 11 reveals Paul's disgust at a degeneration occurring in the church; the isolated people were present, and all were obviously going to be talking about Jesus at the end of the evening; however, they were ignoring the central instruction about eating together. Instead, some were hoarding their food, leaving the poor and liminal people standing unfed and excluded from the table. Paul was livid. While it might have been a Roman thing to stratify the crowd, it certainly was not a Jesus-family thing. Paul's correction, then, was to take them back to that first Lord's Supper and remind them exactly what Jesus initiated. After all, that was what they were practicing—the New Passover.

---

2. Snyder, Hills, and Gardner, *Common Life*, 171.
3. Sweet, *From Tablet to Table*, 14.

The Age-Old Pattern

Jesus' understanding of the table came from something historic. It started in the garden and has continued in hundreds of ways. Leonard Sweet says that the first command of God in the garden is to eat freely; the last command in Revelation is to drink freely; everything in between is more tables where we eat with God and each other.[4] But a more specific breakdown reveals God using meals for the Abrahamic covenant, the Passover meal, and other feast remembrances. Beyond that, even the organization of the tabernacle and temple included the table in the Holy Place with its goblets, bowls, and serving utensils. The imagery is rich and reveals a divine commitment to the table as a place for sacred union between the creator and the created. All in all, these Old Testament usages of table forged a culture of holy hospitality among the Jews. This was the culture into which Jesus was born.

The Jesus Table

Today, theologians are scrambling to embrace Jesus' prominent and strategic use of the table in his salvific mission. The size and scope of the Jesus table has only recently been brought to the forefront, thanks to the work of Dennis E. Smith, Hal Taussig, and Matthias Klinghardt in 2003.[5] Theologian and author Alan Streett highlights how their research has built a convincing case that the Lord's Supper was not only a full meal but followed the structure of a two-course Roman banquet.[6] The theological world

---

4. Mike Graves, *Table Talk: Rethinking Communion and Community* (Eugene, OR: Cascade, 2017), 131.

5. Dennis E. Smith, Hal Taussig, and Matthias Klinghardt, *From Symposium to Eucharist: The Banquet in the Early Christian World* (Minneapolis: Fortress, 2003).

6. Streett, *Subversive Meals*, 2.

that had contextualized Jesus' narratives in the Jewish world were now faced with the reality that there had not been sufficient theological reflection on the impact of the Roman world on the Jews. Before 2003, most scholars followed Hans Leitzmann's proposals that the agape and symbolic eucharist were separate events. But after Smith's groundbreaking research, only a small minority now hold to separation of agape and Eucharist.[7] This is important because is it helps us interpret the Gospel verses about Jesus at tables as something more than the routine of mealtime, but rather an intentional strategy with spiritual designs. Specifically, the Dinner Church movement that is occurring today finds its deepest roots in that Last Supper of the first Holy Week.

The Zacchaeus Example

Having established the consistency with which Jesus pursued the table makes one wonder what he talked about between bites of fish and flatbread. One of the great encounters that gives insight into Jesus' table conversation was when he invited himself over to Zacchaeus' house (Luke 19). To step back a moment, Zacchaeus was a Jew who was hated because he collected taxes for the oppressive Roman regime. He was also short in stature. The culmination of his social rejection and biological reality drove him into a tree to get a glimpse of the miracle worker. The crowd would never cooperate to allow him to get close enough to see, yet there was an obvious spiritual yearning. Jesus looked up at this well-dressed man in a tree and discerned the state of Zacchaeus' vacuous soul. Jesus just couldn't walk by someone who "already knew they were

---

7. Streett, *Subversive Meals*, 2.

a sinner."[8] When they got to Zacchaeus' house, what unfolds is a conversation that should serve as a model of table talk for every Christ follower.

According to Luke 19:7, everyone knew Zacchaeus was a thief and referred to him as a notorious sinner. Yet Jesus never treated him as anything but a friend and even honored him by going to his house. I have heard some writers suppose that Jesus must have said some things that brought a sense of conviction to Zacchaeus because of the way he confessed his wrongdoings. But that is an argument from textual absence. The only thing we see in the gospel narrative is Jesus and his disciples enjoying the meal with Zacchaeus, which was the customary hospitality of the day. Then Zacchaeus stood up, interrupted the mealtime chatter, and admitted he was a cheat and a thief. He then promised to pay back those he had cheated and committed to start using his wealth to lift the poor. It was Zacchaeus who deepened the conversation, after which Jesus simply replied, "Today, salvation has come to this house" (Luke 19:9). There is a timely lesson to be learned here: when we are at Jesus tables, we do not have to force a spiritual conversation with secular people, they will. Jesus tables in which Jesus Stories are preached usher in Jesus' presence. And that will prompt a desire in people to talk about spiritual things, just like it did in Zacchaeus.

Table Talk

Beyond the Zacchaeus story, a huge percentage of the Gospels has captured Jesus and the disciples engaging in table talk. Many

---

8.   This reference is repeated in all three synoptic Gospels: Matthew 9:13; Mark 2:17; Luke 5:32.

theologians have started noting this as of late. Mike Graves states that on nearly every page in the book of Luke, Jesus is either going to a meal, at a meal, or coming from a meal.[9] Marcus Barth estimates that meals account for nearly one-fifth of all verses found in Luke and Acts.[10] Leonard Sweet adds, "Of the 23 parables in Luke's Gospel, more than fifteen of them feature food (70%)."[11] So thick is Luke's mealtime focus that Robert Karris wrote an entire book on the subject, titled "Eating Your Way Through Luke's Gospel."[12] And Daniel Reid concludes that the book of Luke clearly demonstrates that meals were an assumed context for Jesus' teaching.[13] In other words, no one would go to a meal with Jesus present without expecting him to teach as the meal concluded.

There has been a lot of scholarship on the topic of Jesus talk at Jesus tables. It has been assumed that much of Jesus' teaching happened along the shores of Galilee when much of it was happening around a table. Present at these Jesus tables were sinners and saints and religious leaders and disciples and the poor and prostitutes and all sorts of wanted and unwanted people. It was at these Christian meals that Jesus welcomed sinners into his kingdom and offered them a forecast of heaven's joys.[14] I doubt anyone would question if the topic of the kingdom of heaven came up at these tables. It would be hard not to conclude that God's kingdom literally flowed out from the table.[15]

---

9. Graves, *Table Talk*, 40.
10. Streett, *Subversive Meals*, 131.
11. Sweet, *From Tablet to Table*, 110.
12. Robert J. Karris, *Eating Your Way Through Luke's Gospel* (Collegeville, MN: Liturgical Press, 2006.
13. Daniel Reid, *Dictionary of the New Testament* (Westmont, IL: InterVarsity Press, 2004), 4.
14. Streett, *Subversive Meals*, 170.
15. David Fitch and Geoff Holsclaw, *Prodigal Christianity: 10 Signposts into the Missional Frontier* (San Francisco: Jossey-Bass, 2013), 97.

Along with kingdom talk at these tables, many questions were asked of Jesus. Christian author J. R. Briggs says that Jesus was asked 187 questions in the Gospels.[16] Many of those were predictably at tables, due to the social opportunity to recline, think, and process spiritual issues. Jesus usually answered a question with another question. In this way he demonstrated mastery in prompting vibrant dialogue. These Christian banquets initiated by Jesus and continued by his disciples were a dynamic smorgasbord of supernatural activity: prophecies, revelations, words of knowledge, healings, and miracles, each producing a profound effect on the participants—giving them a foretaste of the kingdom to come.[17]

The Ministry of Reconciliation

In 2 Corinthians 5:18, Paul spoke of the church being given the ministry of reconciliation. The context of these words focused on reconciliation to God. However, I would propose that the patterns learned from divine reconciliation are the same for human reconciliation. I see this fusion in 1 Peter 3:7, where husbands are told to be considerate of their wives so that their prayers will not be hindered. In other words, our paths of reconciliation toward humanity affects our reconciliation toward the divine. We only have one heart with which to love. The way we nurture our earthly relationships is the way we nurture our divine relationship. The way we reconcile the heavenly relationship is the way we reconcile our earthly relationships.

We live at a time when society needs the church to be well-practiced at the ministry of reconciliation. Racial divisions, politi-

---

16. J. R. Briggs, Live Lecture at Missio Conference, Alexandria, VA, March 28, 2019.

17. Streett, *Subversive Meals*, 243–44.

cal divisions, and classist divisions are ripping at the very fabric of our nation. The spirit of division is an all-consuming cancer that is affecting everyone. To this deep challenge stands one historic answer: the Jesus table and the Jesus Stories. There is a unique and divine ability infused into these New Passovers that are not paralleled in other social settings. Augustine commented that there is no ultimate harmonization of differences until the coming of the heavenly city.[18] However, the church is called to embody that unity as a vision for society. Unfortunately, we have pulled all the salt out of our neighborhoods and brought them into safe, hermetically sealed churches.[19] Our world is divided and in trouble, but the church has an answer. We know the path to reconciliation.

History records that President Lincoln once met a disfavorable political opponent and later commented, "I do not like that man; I must invite him to dinner." He understood the power of the table to create common ground. Jesus tables start with the communal potential of gathering around food but amplify it with such a divine spirit of reconciliation that they heal broken relationships and blend the hearts of very different people. Jesus tables and Jesus Stories have natural blending capacities that are simply not found in other sectors of society. It is the church's singular opportunity to offer.

An important distinction needs to be made: it is not as likely that we can reconcile opposing groups as much as we can reconcile individual people through Jesus' table fellowship. In Jesus' day two primary narratives existed: the Roman dominance narrative and the historic Judaism narrative. His response to this emotional

---

18. D. A. Carson, *Christ and Culture Revisited* (Grand Rapids, MI: Eerdmans, 2008), 177.

19. Carson, *Christ and Culture Revisited*, 214.

division was to plant an alternate narrative altogether: the kingdom of heaven. Today we are in a similar position: we have people traversing ideological paths that are completely dis-unifiable from other people holding to opposite ideological paths (red vs. blue, ethnic pain vs. societal central, the haves vs. the have-nots). But when we bring different people together around a Jesus table and discuss Jesus Stories, something remarkable happens: brotherhood and sisterhood starts to form. In no time folks are eating together, laughing together, and even praying together. It is the history of the church, the nature of *koinonia*, and the assignment of the *kerygma* to bring people together around Jesus' alternate story of the inbreaking kingdom. It is as beautiful as it is surprising. And yet, it is exactly what Ivan Illich said: "If you want to change society, you must tell an alternate story."[20]

Brian McLaren recalls that the work of racial reconciliation was barely a footnote to the gospel he grew up hearing.[21] I join him in that reflection. The churches I attended were resolutely focused on Bible teaching, but only vaguely focused on the implications of societal reconciliation. They dealt with unity and reconciliation within the Christian community but somehow never applied those scriptural principles to helping fractured groups in society come together. Most churches have similarly overlooked the ministry of reconciliation, yet it is a huge door into their cities. The church must step into this ministry, especially since we have actual answers to offer.

Methodist leader Stephanie Moore-Hand states that racism is resolved by Christian discipleship. The biblical text points the

---

20. Leonard Sweet, Andy Crouch, Michael Horton, and Frederica Mathewes-Green, *The Church in Emerging Culture* (Grand Rapids, MI: Zondervan, 2003), 33.

21. Sweet et al., *The Church in Emerging Culture*, 213

way, from the Great Commission that calls us to be Jesus' witnesses to all people, to the book of Revelation that reveals those gathered in heaven will be from every tongue and tribe and people and nation.[22] And together we all will eat the marriage supper of the lamb (Rev. 5:9; 19:9). There are many scriptures and Jesus Stories that make it impossible to embrace any form of racial bias and at the same time be a mature Christ-follower. Encasing the ministry of reconciliation into the role of discipleship is profoundly helpful. It clarifies an important developmental point of Christlike formation, and it connects scripture and the Jesus Stories to the actual cause of reconciliation. If Christian discipleship dissolves racism and Christian discipleship is based on the written word and the Living Word, the Jesus Stories create racial reconciliation. This means that Jesus Stories and Jesus tables place us back in the center of society's painful divisions with the ministry of reconciliation in our hands.

We should be great at this peacemaking role; we understand the Jesus table and we understand the Jesus Stories. The combination of the two makes us unbelievably winsome at turning diverse people into a warm family. Theologian and author Dan Allender states, "A leader is first a storyteller: telling a story of their foolishness, and then of their redemption, reconciliation, and restoration."[23] Despite society's attempts to sideline us, we can show up for them with food on our tables, the Jesus Stories on our lips, and the ministry of reconciliation in our hands. We can do this, church! We can help society heal! Consider the sentiment

---

22. Stephanie Moore-Hand, "Racism and the Local Church" (Lecture, Exponential Conference, First Baptist Church, Orlando, FL, March 8, 2022).

23. Dan Allender, *Leading with a Limp* (Colorado Springs: Waterbrook, 2006), 153.

of Edwin Markham's poem: "They drew a circle and shut us out
. . . we drew another circle and took them in!"[24]

The Revelatory Moment

The combination of Jesus Stories at Jesus tables creates open-heaven experiences on earth. We saw this after the resurrection when Jesus joined two of his followers as they were walking to Emmaus (Luke 24). They had been discussing the crucifixion and disappearance of Jesus after the tomb had been found open. They were very disturbed by these occurrences. When Jesus entered the conversation, he pointed out key passages from the scriptures to inspire their faith. Then, as it was nearing dinnertime, they stopped at Emmaus to eat; there at the table Jesus took the bread, blessed it, broke it, and gave it to them. And suddenly, their eyes opened, and they recognized him. Once they saw it was Jesus, he disappeared from right in front of them.

Let us pause for a moment and acknowledge that they did not recognize Jesus on the road, though he was revealing prophetic truth to them about the events that had just occurred in Jerusalem. But when they sat at the table and broke bread with Jesus, their eyes were suddenly opened, and they saw him alive and well. The table provided an opportunity for a revelatory moment; on the road Jesus reasoned with them, but it wasn't until he ate with them that the scales of grief fell away, and they were able to see the living Jesus in living color. That is what Jesus tables are all about: they are a place where Jesus loves to reveal himself to human hearts. As church father Jerome wrote to Nepotian, "Let poor persons and strangers be acquainted with your modest table,

---

24. Edwin Markham, "Outwitted," epigram.

and with them Christ shall be your guest."[25] We cannot withhold the presence of Jesus at these Jesus tables. Understanding the revelatory nature of Jesus tables helps us understand the role of the Jesus Stories.

Let us consider something else that happened in Emmaus that day. Jesus punctuated the importance of his self-revelation with another mystery; he disappeared from the table. One moment he was sitting there eating bread, and the next moment he was gone! The point was made; Jesus was alive; he took them to a table to reveal himself; and as mysteriously as he opened their eyes he disappeared from their sight. This was about as big of a mic drop as the ascension would prove to be a few days later. But remember, the Emmaus story became noteworthy because of what happened at a table. There is a hand-in-glove relationship here; understanding the links between tables and stories and Jesus revelations may not be logical, but they are real. And they repeat themselves over and over to this very day. Emmaus was not the last of the Jesus table mysteries.

My wife, Melodee, developed a friendship with a young woman at one of our dinner churches in Seattle. This gal had fled a life of rejection on the East Coast but all too quickly found herself living in her car in our city. After attending for several months, she came up to Melodee one night, held up her plate of food, and said, "Look at this! I know you see food, but I see life." My wife had watched the Lord drawing this young woman to himself in the warmest of ways over the months. But on that night, she saw Jesus in that plate of food, and it overwhelmed her. Remembering Jesus while sitting at one of his tables produces re-

---

25.   Jerome's Letter 52, quoted in Ben Witherington III, *Making a Meal of It* (Waco, TX: Baylor University Press, 2007), 87.

markable spiritual fruit; Jesus tables and Jesus Stories usher Jesus' presence into the human soul. The mystery of how Jesus reveals himself that was seen in Emmaus repeats itself over and over, and it will repeat itself in the hearts of your table guests too.

Practical Approaches

It is time for you to witness a Jesus revelation in real time. Find a dinner church near you to visit and sit next to someone who probably would never visit your Sunday church. Ask them a few questions about their life and tell them a bit about your life. When the Jesus Story is preached, listen with your heart how Jesus might be revealing himself to people's hearts in the room? How might he be revealing himself to your new friend?

Let that insight direct your prayer over the next week. And if you can visit again, sit by that same person, and grow the friendship even deeper. And again, discern how Jesus is revealing himself. After a few weeks you will come to the conclusion that you are witnessing revelatory moments—Jesus introducing himself to lost hearts.

Offer My Favor—to the Poor, the Blind, the Oppressed

Another directive from our Lord to prioritize his words occurs during the reading of his mission statement before his hometown crowd. Luke 4 records that Jesus walked into the Jewish meeting place in Nazareth and was asked to do the reading. While everyone watched, Jesus unrolled the scroll of Isaiah to the section that says, "The Spirit of the Lord is upon me, because he has anointed me to proclaim good news to the poor. He has sent me to proclaim freedom for the prisoners and recovery of sight for the blind, to set the oppressed free, to proclaim the year of the Lord's favor" (Luke 4:18 NIV). Then he rolled up the scroll, handed it back to the attendant, and told the listeners how that reading was becoming fulfilled that very day. He was giving this crowd his commission at the onset of his ministry. In overview, it is obvious that Jesus' divine calling was to pursue the poor, the captives, the blind, and the oppressed. But the message that was to be repeated the most throughout Jesus' ministry was proclaiming the good news to the poor. We see an example of this in Matthew 11:4 when John the Baptist sent his disciples to inquire if Jesus was indeed the Messiah. Jesus' answer to them was to go back and tell John that the blind are being healed and the gospel is being preached to the poor. That was proof that he knew John would recognize.

While we will be discussing preaching in a later chapter, it is here we consider the audience Jesus longed to pursue. In fact, Jesus' version of preaching assumed a particular audience would be present. Thus, Jesus' many directives to his disciples to go preach the gospel assumed a similar audience would be sought and would be present. Let me be clear: Jesus has directed us to pour his words, his teaching, and his stories into the lives of the poor, the sick, the oppressed, and the stranger.

A History of Stranger-Care

A disturbing story is found in Judges 19, where a man and those traveling with him stopped at a Jebusite town to spend the night. A local elderly man coming home for the evening saw these strangers readying themselves to bed down in the town square. Somehow, this party was overlooked by the town elders, who were left to fend for themselves.[1] When the elderly man saw the encampment, he asked them to come home with him because it was not safe to stay in the town square. But during the night a crowd of troublemakers beat on the old man's door and demanded he turn over his guests to them. The old man appealed to the mob saying, "This man is a guest in my house, and such a thing would be shameful." The rest of the story is difficult to read. But notice the deep culture of caring for the stranger that was present in that premodern village. The elderly man felt an obligation to protect the strangers that were in his home. In fact, he incurred huge costs

---

1. Eric Jacobsen, *The Space Between: A Christian Engagement with the Built Environment* (Grand Rapids, MI: Baker Academic, 2012), 248.

that night. Caring for the stranger was assumed throughout the tribes of Israel; it was foundational in their culture and theology.

Have you given much thought to the need for the church in the West to shift its treatment of the stranger? According to Christian author Eric Jacobsen, the Bible has a well-developed theology of "the stranger."[2] I propose church leaders in the West need to spend more time evaluating this topic. I do not make this appeal solely because of a theological oversight, but because we live in a day when isolation and estrangement is reaching choking volumes in our country. Theologian and professor Christine Pohl reports that large numbers of refugees fleeing persecution during the sixteenth century drove a significant resurgence of the moral responsibility to lift the needy strangers.[3] Similar realities are flooding the developed world today.

Society needs a church that can embrace all the liminal people again—those isolated ones who have no helper to sustain them. Theology professor David Lim reveals the Greek word for hospitality in the New Testament—*philoxenoi*—which literally means a love for strangers solely because of their disconnectedness.[4] Though much of the church has drifted into the congregation business in recent centuries, regaining a christological theology of the stranger is possible.

Stranger Stories

Many of Jesus' stories are based on the culture and theology of stranger care. In Luke 11, Jesus told a parable about a man who

2. Jacobsen, 243.
3. Christine Pohl, *Making Room: Recovering Hospitality as a Christian Tradition* (Grand Rapids, MI: Eerdmans, 1999), 52.
4. David Lim, *Spiritual Gifts* (Springfield, MO: Gospel Publishing House, 2003), 207.

had guests arrive during the evening. The host, being low on food, went to his neighbor to borrow some bread. His neighbor protested because his own family was already in bed, but the host kept knocking until his neighbor got up and gave him what he needed. While the message was about persistence in prayer, it also demonstrated how culturally unacceptable it would be to have guests and not feed them. Even if the guest showed up unexpectedly in the middle of the night, Middle Eastern hospitality would demand that food be offered.

In Luke 10, Jesus told another parable about the traveler who had been attacked, beaten, robbed, and left injured on the road by bandits. A priest came along but did not want to put himself in danger, so he crossed to the other side of the road and hurried along without helping the injured man. Then a temple assistant came by who at least stopped and looked at him but then decided not to get involved. Finally, a despised Samaritan came down that road, saw the wounded traveler, felt compassion for him, soothed his injuries with olive oil and bandages, put him on his own donkey, took him to an inn at the next town, and paid for the room so the stranger could heal. This story was told about the religious leaders, to point out their reluctance to practice the theology of the stranger. But Jesus piled on extra coals of condemnation by presenting a despised Samaritan as the one who upstaged the religious leaders. Interestingly, it is usually those who have experienced the pains, injuries, isolations, and rejections themselves who are most willing to help others in their time of need. Seasons of abandonment and injury in our lives often become the soil in which the theology of stranger-care grows.

Another set of Jesus Stories that addresses the theology of stranger-care is the triad parables of the lost sheep, the lost coin, and the lost son. Jesus obviously told these stories back-to-back to emphasize his point, like a boxer hitting you with a left, then a right, then a left again. He wanted the hearer to be impacted deeply by this truth. What was his primary point? That the normalness of life needs to be interrupted to care for those who are lost and in need. While many great and rich truths are buried in these three stories, the shared denominators are these: they are all in great need, they are all alone in their struggle, they are all lacking someone to intervene, and they are all strangers. When someone on earth finds him- or herself in that place of need, all of heaven stops to focus on that person. Jesus expects his church to stop and notice them too.

Then in Matthew 25 we hear the most monumental words regarding a lifelong commitment to the stranger. Here Jesus told how one day all humanity will be separated into two groups: One group will be all who cared for the hungry, clothed the naked, cared for the sick, and visited the prisoner. The other group will be those who did not engage in the activities of lifting up the needy. Jesus made it clear that eternity will judge the people of earth on the metric of stranger care. This is quite the lesson for any serious follower of Christ.

Invited to the New Passovers

The Last Supper was a wonderful time for Jesus to have a final moment with his disciples before being arrested. But it was also a time for him to leave them with a vision of doing Christian gatherings after his death, resurrection, and ascension. To do this, he took the Passover, which was an annual remembrance event, and changed it from focusing on Israel's rescue from Egypt to focusing on Jesus himself. He enacted this new understanding with the words, "Remember me." However, one thing Jesus did not change from the original Passover was who should be invited to these New Passovers. The original invite list from Deuteronomy 16:11–12 was still in effect:

> Celebrate with your sons and daughters, your male and female servants, the Levites from your towns, and the foreigners, orphans, and widows who live among you. Remember that you were once slaves in Egypt, so be careful to obey all these decrees.

If there was ever a thorough list of strangers, this would be it. The fact that Jesus changed some of the historic Passover but not the invite list should mean something to us. Jesus wants the strangers at his tables as much as the Father did throughout Israel's feasts. "Heaven seeking strangers" represents a timeless commitment.

The First-Sought Population

The ministry of Jesus unapologetically reached out for those who did not have a community around them. Strangers have always created a social situation for towns. We always have people with us who have become disconnected from their families, friends, and townspeople due to travel or negative life circumstances.

When Jesus sent out his disciples two-by-two, he instructed them to pursue the at-risk population with healing and invitations into the kingdom of heaven. He was directing them toward the same audiences he pursued. There was a lot of poverty and difficulty in the land during those days of Roman rule. Alan Streett reports that 90 percent of the population was of the peasant class, and the Roman elites leveraged excessive taxes on these lower-classed people, which kept them poor.[5] This was the social situation Jesus and his disciples encountered throughout their ministry.

Following the resurrection of Christ, the disciples continued to face these impoverished factors. Greco-Roman cities were extremely crowded, filthy, disorderly, filled with strangers, and afflicted. More people per acre lived in ancient Antioch than live currently in Calcutta.[6] So when Acts 6 records Antioch's efforts to care for the widows and organize deacons to run the huge table ministries for these liminal people, it was a big response to a big need. It was their strength to rise to the task that made the Antioch Church the sending center of the gospel for a long while. We dare not take this vision of the stranger lightly. Could this be a reason why many churches have lost their missional heartbeat?

Rule of Hospitality

The Jesus Stories had a powerful impact on Saint Benedict, especially the ones focused on the stranger. Benedict, an Italian reformer known as the father of Western monasticism, established *The Rule of St. Benedict* in 480 CE. Benedict's Rule became a pattern for optimal spiritual formation and one of the great turning points in Christian history.[7] The Rule had over ninety prescribed practices.[8] But, it is the Rule of Hospitality that has rung ever so loudly through the centuries: "The stranger is received as Christ, welcomed warmly, and invited into prayer, the reading of the

---

5. Streett, *Subversive Meals*, 91.

6. Chuck Lawless and Adam Greenway, T*he Great Commission Resurgence: Fulfilling God's Mandate In Our Time* (Nashville: B&H, 2010), 309.

7. James Emery White, *Serious Times* (Downers Grove, IL: InterVarsity, 2004), 94.

8. Alan Hirsch and Dave Ferguson, *On the Verge: A Journey into the Apostolic Future of the Church* (Grand Rapids, MI: Zondervan, 2011), 181.

scripture, and a shared meal."[9] Some believe this was Benedict's way of continuing what Jesus started by feeding the 5,000, and the 4,000, and the early church's Agape meals.[10] In other words, Benedict's Rule was based on the Jesus Stories and the Jesus tables.

While many stories dot the landscape of Christian history showing how Jesus Stories have prompted a theology of the stranger, one is unusually compelling. In 1785, a group of Methodists, with the support of John Wesley, founded the Strangers Friend Society in London. According to author Christine Pohl, these societies were dedicated to ministry among the urban poor that they described as strangers because of their inability to find relief and because they had no helper in society.[11] Similar to the Benedictine monks, they sent Christians into English cities to turn strangers into friends around tables.

We can see a natural union between stranger-care and the table. This is not only beneficial for the stranger, but also for Christlike formation. American theologian Richard Mouw talks about how the best training grounds for learning how to deal with people who are different from us, or even annoying to us, is a dinner table.[12] The routine of eating together forms a bond around those tables. There is an Afghan saying, "Here we drink three cups of tea; the first you are a stranger, the second you are a friend, and the third you join our family."[13] The Christian table has experienced similar progressions as strangers became family around food. The Benedictine Rule and the Strangers Friend So-

---

9. Pohl, *Making Room*, 96.

10. Elizabeth Newman, *Untamed Hospitality* (Grand Rapids, MI: Brazos, 2007), 149.

11. Pohl, *Making Room*, 88.

12. Jacobsen, *The Space Between*, 154.

13. Neil Johnson, *Business as Mission* (Downers Grove, IL: InterVarsity, 2009), 315.

cieties and others have served as rich examples of what happens when a group allows the Jesus Stories to shape a theology of the stranger within them.

Strangers and the Local Church

Some years ago, several graduate students from my seminary were invited to meet with the eighteen executive presbyters of the Assemblies of God. It was an honor to be in the room and listen to the issues they were discussing. Then at lunchtime we were seated among those leaders to speak with them in a personal way. It was there that I met the long-time pastor of a large Assemblies of God congregation in Texas. He started sharing how his church had plateaued for over twenty years. Though it was still a mega-church, he was broken-hearted at his inability to reach more of his city. He tried many things to get it growing again—moving the campus, enlisting a strategic turnaround process, starting a twenty-four-hour prayer initiative—and still they remained stalled. Then came a breakthrough for his church; it happened once they started reaching for the broken population in their city. And though he had to fire a few leaders who did not like the new direction, their church nearly doubled in size; they were back on mission.

Any group that reaches for the estranged, the isolated, the least, the lost, the last, the left-behind, and the stranger are aligning to Jesus' version of stranger care. The raw percentage of Jesus' stories that focus on the stranger should spur us to create a large place in our theology and ecclesial practices. When Jesus directed us to proclaim the good news, it assumed a particular audience would be present—the least, the last, the lost, and the left-behind.

Recovering Stranger-Care

Historically, the Christian story has had a preferential eye for the stranger. Aristades described Christians to the Roman emperor Hadrian this way: "They love one another; they never fail to help widows; they save orphans from those who would hurt them; if they have something they give freely to the man who has nothing; if they see a stranger, they take him home, and are happy, as though he were a real brother."[14] What a beautiful report of our heritage chronicled in governmental records.

While it appears that we have slipped from that ideal, I am watching a renewed eye for the stranger emerge in many churches. While some of this is due to the work of Fresh Expressions, as well as the Dinner Church movements,[15] I think a lot of it is the natural progression of the Lausanne movement that started in July 1974 in Switzerland. There, a convocation of the world's theologians gathered from 150 nations to wrestle with the decline of the church. Great names like Billy Graham, Samuel Escobar, Francis Schaeffer, Carl Henry, John Stott, and Ralph Winters were among the leaders of this conversation. At the end of the convocation, the Lausanne Covenant was forged around this premise: "Never again shall the proclamation of the Gospel be conceived as un-welded from Social Engagement in equal measure."[16]

---

14. Rick Rusaw and Eric Swanson, *The Externally Focused Church* (Loveland, CO: Group Publishing, 2004), 58.

15. Fresh Expressions is a movement that began among the Anglicans in the United Kingdom in 2008 and moved to the United States in 2012. It has been effective in planting new faith communities among those who do not do church. The dinner church movement began in 2007 and joined Fresh Expressions in 2016. It has been effective in gathering secular people around historic Jesus tables. They are also known as agape tables, New Passovers, and dinner churches.

16. Wonsok Ma, *The Shelf Life of Christianity* (lecture, Oxford Centre for Missions Studies, Oxford, UK, March 2, 2010).

The Lausanne Covenant worked a wonder in that it merged the church's definition of the gospel. Traditional churches had practiced the social gospel, which did many helpful works but excluded proclamation. On the other hand, the Evangelical Church loudly proclaimed the gospel but ignored the social needs around them. This covenant brought the two lanes into one, and the church in the West has been moving toward that fuller definition of the gospel ever since. The Lausanne movement has continued to host world convocations through the years in Manila, Cape Town, and would have met in Wilsa, Poland, had it not been interrupted by the pandemic. In overview, the Lausanne Covenant birthed and nurtured a fully orbed definition of the gospel, enabling the church to preach to the human soul, restore the neighborhood, and embrace the stranger.

While the Dinner Church movement was raised up by the Spirit from the four corners of the land, our story in Seattle quickly revealed a deep relationship with the strangers in our city. If you were to attend any of our dinner churches, you'd watch the pastor remind the leaders and volunteers beforehand that the most important job in the room that night was turning strangers into friends. In Seattle, everyone is expected to grab a plate, sit down next to someone new, and turn them into a friend. I have now observed other dinner churches across the country giving that speech in a dozen different ways. In fact, the Dinner Church movement cannot be understood without prioritizing the stranger, the sick, the oppressed, and the poor.

Practical Approaches

Practicing stranger-care is difficult in most churches, but it is natural with dinner churches. Can you start a Jesus Table? If you are unable to start one, find another ministry or social-lifting nonprofit to join. Union Gospel Missions, Dream Centers, and food banks are all good places to look. However, don't just serve food or hand out supplies. Find a way to sit down with strangers long enough and often enough to make a friend out of them. Remember, if they are friends with you, they are only inches away from being friends with the Jesus, who lives in you. Consult the national map to find a dinner church near you at www.DinnerChurch.Com/Locations.

Be Witnesses to Me—
Tell My Stories

Another clear directive Jesus gave us to prioritize his words and content comes from Luke's remembrance of the Great Commission: "And you shall be witnesses to me, telling people about me everywhere—in Jerusalem, throughout Judea, in Samaria, and to the ends of the earth" (Acts 1:8). This verse is the most repeated authorization for witnessing and personal evangelism. And yet, Reformation-era Christians have somehow side-stepped Jesus' request and focused on being witnesses to many other things besides the life of Christ. But Jesus only asked us to be witnesses to one thing: his life and words and stories.

If we witnessed an automobile accident and a police officer asked us to tell what we witnessed, we would talk about the accident as it unfolded. We would not drift into the color of the house nearby, or the age of the tree on the corner, or the make and model of our car back home. That would be ludicrous. And yet, present-day Christians have turned witnessing into an apologetic of all scripture rather than doing what Jesus asked—be witnesses to his life. Interesting. We have gone so far as to develop outlines like The Romans Road to Salvation, Evangelism Explosion, and other dialogues. These constructs sound good to us, but they aren't what Jesus asked us to do. Consequently, the winsome and compelling life of Jesus has been coopted by modernist outlines, which has left us incapable of having meaningful discussions about faith with secular people. The church of Jesus needs the stories of Jesus to become *the* definition of the good news once again.

Personal evangelism in our day has proved to be very hard for most Christians. Those who have delved deeply into the ennea-gram, Myers-Briggs, or other personality studies quickly realize that only a portion of the human spectrum is naturally effective in confrontative environments. Thus, evangelism as is commonly conceived places 75 percent of the body of Christ on the bench due to their personality formation and gifting alignments. No wonder 99 out of 100 churches across the denominational spectrum are un-able to replace their attrition by reaching the secular lost.[1] But once we define witnessing as retelling the Jesus Stories, any believer can become a vibrant witness to the life of Jesus by telling the stories of Jesus. E. G. Selwyn points out that the term for witness (*marturian*) is used six times more frequently in the New Testament than the term for preaching (*kerygma*).[2] This tells me that Jesus expected his stories to gain traction in every culture throughout all time, and that anyone can be a witness about his life stories.

Hell Guy

A couple of years ago Melodee and I were on a flight when she overheard a conversation in the row in front of us. A young man in his twenties was seated next to a middle-aged man who was clearly a Christian on a mission. The conversation started off okay as the Christian man engaged the younger one by asking about his life. This young man talked about his heavy metal garage band

---

1.   John Bishop quoting Andy McAdams, *Dangerous Church: Risking Everything to Reach Everyone* (Grand Rapids, MI: Zondervan, 2011), 39.

2.   Fitch and Holsclaw, *Prodigal Christianity*, 59.

and how he was having fun making music with his friends. The Christian man was friendly and laughed at a couple points. But as the plane began to descend, the pressure to close the deal began to mount, and a new tone overtook the conversation. The Christian man started talking about faith and God, and was obviously following an evangelism outline of sorts. Then after the plane landed, he stood to wrestle down his luggage and turned back to the young man to drop the final hammer: "Son, anyone who does not confess their sins and accept the Savior is going to hell. Now you don't want to go to hell, do you?" Then he turned to deplane, happy that he had delivered the gospel. Melodee was livid. This turned out to be one of the worst attempts to engage an evangelistic moment that she had seen in years. I almost had to restrain my wife from confronting the man and berating him for the damage he had inflicted on this poor unsuspecting echomillennial. We looked for that young man in the terminal to try to restore a sibilance of the actual good news, but we could not find him. But it became a high watermark for how contrived and coercive our modernist versions of witnessing can sound.

The explanation of the gospel that sounds so right to us is often anything but good news to our unreached neighbors. By contrast, the Jesus Stories that are driven along by the Spirit within us creates a completely different conversation. Rather than confronting the sinner, they intrigue the mind and warm the heart until Jesus himself shows up and a divine friendship is born. Now *that* is the good news.

The Nature of Sin

We cannot begin to comprehend the nature of evangelism until we are reminded about the nature of sin. Throughout history, humans have demonstrated a talent for turning heavenly wisdom into rules and regulations. We do this so we can categorize and control our spirituality. We'd rather grab God than trust God to grab us. Religious leaders in Jesus' day were notorious for doing this, but we have done it, too, when it comes to the topic of sin. Present practices have reduced sin and salvation to a choice. I know Adam and Eve chose to eat from the forbidden tree, but does that explain the full nature of sin?

I am intrigued by what happened to Israel in the Negev Desert when the snakes came out and bit the people because of their grumbling. In response, God directed Moses to make an image of a snake and put it on a pole. Anyone who looked at that image was healed. While it was a difficult day for the people of God, it demonstrated how sin was like poison. Further, it revealed what the antidote would look like when it comes, which the world witnessed as Jesus was lifted on the cross. On that day he became the antidote to rid the most elemental problem affecting this world: soul poison. Greed, lust, selfishness, fear, and attacking others are just a few of the poisons that destroy our lives, our families, our neighborhoods, our cities, our government, and the world around us. The very mention of the name of Jesus releases the antidote and counteracts the poison in the human soul.

Seventy years ago, one of my family members was bitten by a rattle snake. He lay in a field for over an hour in the heat of a summer day, and by the time others found him, he was in a bad way. Had a doctor been there and seen his delirious state, he would have taken charge and administered the antidote. After all, this man was in no state to decide anything; the poison had rendered him incapacitated. To talk of salvation only in terms of a choice is shortsighted. This, then, is the nature of sin. It poisons us. This, then, must be the nature of evangelism—to freely dispense the antidote. Every time we speak of Jesus and tell his stories, the antidote goes to work. There might be a day when a sin-poisoned person can choose to welcome Jesus into his or her life, but we need to start delivering the antidote long before that time. The church today needs a deeper vision of the nature of sin so that we can embrace a deeper vision of the antidote that is in our hands—the antidote revealed by the Jesus Stories.

The Apologetics Problem

While I enjoy the rationality of apologetics, there is a problem when it comes to evangelism. Unfortunately, the leading ideas of evangelism usually cause believers to feel they must wrestle people away from their secular belief systems and accept the superior belief system of Christianity. Thus, there exists an emphasis on verbal techniques and questions drawn from the either/or world of apologetics.

Interestingly, the term *apologetics* was only recently crafted, but all too quickly it has become the foundation of modern evangelism. The gospel has suffered as a result. Christian author Ron Martoia states that apologetics was an enterprise largely built around the scientific model of garnering evidence for the purpose of persuasion.[3] But that is what we rationalists do with everything. We have managed to turn art, sports, and, yes, Christianity into scientific models. US Senate chaplain Barry Black states, "Christianity was born in the Middle East as a religion; moved to

---

3.   Ron Martoia, *Transformational Architecture* (Grand Rapids, MI: Zondervan, 2008), 142.

Greece and became a philosophy; journeyed to Rome and became a legal system; spread through Europe as a culture; and when it migrated to America Christianity became big business."[4] Ouch. Most leaders do not want their churches to be big businesses built on models and apologetics, but it is almost unavoidable these days. Pastors are trained in it, congregants want it, and almost every conference venerates it.

We have reached a breaking point, as evidenced by our inability to win our secular neighbors to Christ. According to theologian Todd Hunter, "We got the Gospel wrong; we were telling the story of modernity and baby boom aspirations rather than the radical message of the kingdom."[5] And how did we get that story wrong? Where did we go off the tracks? Martoia believes that rationalists' apologetics, birthed largely in the 1970s, is to blame.[6] The churches that have adjusted their beliefs and practices to align with modernity are in decline.[7] While that might sound like a setback, I'm not so sure. Modernity has not been particularly kind to the Christian faith; it has squeezed out all the mystery and replaced it with propositions and rationales. Modernity has awakened to its own nakedness.[8]

A large world of gospel effectiveness exists beyond bullet points and belief systems. Christian philosopher Myron Penner says that the first order of Christian discourse is the *kerygma*, not

---

4. Barry Black, *From the Hood to the Hill* (Nashville: Thomas Nelson, 2006), 83.

5. Eddie Gibbs and Ryan Bolger, *Emerging Churches* (Grand Rapids, MI: Baker Academic, 2005), 49.

6. Martoia, *Transformational Architecture*, 174.

7. Lesslie Newbigin, *The Gospel in a Pluralist Society* (Grand Rapids, MI: Eerdmans, 1989), 212.

8. Myron Penner, *Christianity and the Postmodern Turn* (Grand Rapids, MI: Baker, 2005), 77.

apologetics.[9] In other words, the Jesus Stories are the first thing Christians should be talking about, not memorized belief-system talking points. Some futurists say that the new apologetics will be an unapologetics.[10] It is interesting to imagine that evangelism in post-Christian America might look almost opposite of our present practices. New generations of Christians will be given a choice to shift from bullet-point evangelism to story-form evangelism, and by that I mean Jesus Story evangelism. The latter approach more naturally employs introverts—those who never felt they had the personality strength to direct a formatted gospel—to join the conversation. The church could surely benefit from everyone in the house capable of sharing the reason for the hope that resides within them. Becoming adept at telling Jesus Stories is what will release the whole family into the whole mission. And with most of our churches in decline, this cannot come too soon.

Reformation Evangelism

I doubt the apostles would recognize the version of evangelism we employ today. Christian author Reggie McNeal says that the primary focus of evangelism today has to do with converting people to church culture.[11] This is a serious degeneration of the original intent. Darrell Guder gives an even worse report that modern churches in North America see evangelism as mere marketing.[12] Marketing and outreaches are certainly shallow ideas of evange-

---

9.   Penner, *Christianity and the Postmodern Turn*, 150.
10.   James Smith, *Who's Afraid of Postmodernism?* (Grand Rapids, MI: Baker, 2006), 74.
11.   Reggie McNeal, *The Missional Renaissance* (San Francisco: Jossey-Bass, 2009), 43.
12.   Darrell Guder, *Missional Church* (Grand Rapids, MI: Eerdmans, 1998), 65.

lism. But we came by these shallow definitions for good reason. It is hard to find any mention of *mission* or *evangelism* in the language of the medieval church; European theology had not dealt with the missionary nature of the church for over 1,000 years.[13]

Throughout US history, we have identified ourselves as Christian America and have handled things like mission and evangelism as an afterthought more than a first calling. It hasn't been until lately that the secular population started to outnumber the Judeo population, and this prompted church leaders to focus more directly on mission. Still, our ideas of evangelism are lagging. Even the move toward Friendship Evangelism, initiated by Rebecca Manly Pippert in the 1980s, has only been a half-measure of the correction needed.[14] While it has offered a refreshing vision of removing evangelism from memorized outlines and instead embedding it into relationship building, it still did not recover the power of the kerygma. At its core, Reformation-era evangelism, as it is practiced today, focuses on getting lost people to pray the sinner's prayer. This idea has not only been ineffective, it has festered into something toxic with the younger generations.

Christian author David Ferguson says that nearly half of Christian millennials believe it is wrong to evangelize, and Christians on average experience two or less faith-oriented conversations with non-Christians in an entire year.[15] Our Reformation-era approaches have led us into a boxed canyon, leaving the church unable to live out the vocation of the Great Commission.

13. Darrell Guder, *The Continuing Conversion of the Church* (Grand Rapids, MI: Eerdmans, 2000), 9.

14. Rebecca Manley Pippert, *Out of the Salt Shaker and into the World* (Downers Grove, IL: InterVarsity, 1979).

15. Dave Ferguson, *Lost Cause: Reviving Evangelism*, Exponential Conference Guide 2022, 182.

A Bounded Past,
a Centered Future

The idea of a bounded set versus centered set was first introduced by anthropologist Paul G. Hiebert in which he proposed that all human groups hold one of two identities: (1) a bounded grouping holding a border of ideas for people to agree with prior to gaining entry, or (2) a centered grouping in which people are included for pursuing a primary idea held at the center without a formal border filtering outsiders from insiders. Hiebert further proposed that most American churches hold a bounded-set identity and needs to shift to a more centered-set identity if they are to be effective in a diverse society. Herbert's call toward centered Christianity has gained significant traction with theologians such as Darrel Guder,[16] Alan Hirsch and Michael Frost,[17] David Livermore,[18] Bob Thune,[19] and, most notably, Phyllis Tickle.[20]

The bounded versus centered conversation identifies a present difficulty for the church, in that leaders are spending an inordinate amount of time teaching and using scripture to guard the borders of the faith. Simply put, people holding a bounded construct read the Bible for a list of theologies to validate and patrol their borders. On the other hand, center-set Christians read scripture to clarify, augment, and enable the vibrant life of Jesus into which we are baptized. Though bounded Christianity has dominated the

---

16.   Guder, *Missional Church*, 206.

17.   Hirsch and Frost, *The Shaping of Things to Come*, 50.

18.   David Livermore *Cultural Intelligence* (Grand Rapids, MI: Baker, 2009), 173.

19.   Bob Thune, "Centered-Set vs. Bounded-Set Churches," accessed January 15, 2024, https://www.bobthune.com/blog/2005/08/bounded-sets-vs-centered-sets.

20.   Phyllis Tickle, The Great Emergence: How Christianity Is Changing and Why (Grand Rapids, MI: Baker, 2012), 159.

church for past centuries, an intersection lies before us—but it is an intersection we have faced before.

In first-century Palestine, the Jewish culture was a bounded group focused on the Law of Moses. But when Jesus arrived, he ignored their ceremonial washings and sabbath rules, he ate with profane people, he befriended sinners, and rather than focusing on their 613 laws he focused on the New Kingdom. In Hiebert's terminology, he moved away from a bounded set of theologies toward a revelation centered on his life and message and kingdom. We see it again when Paul got the gospel ready for the Gentiles who had no history with any law. So rather than talking in right-and-wrong language like Peter used with the Jews, Paul spoke of faith-to-faith, which offered an ever-deepening walk with Jesus— a singular center (see Rom. 1:17). Today, the church is trying to present a right-and-wrong gospel to a secular population that is not wired to appreciate any bounded approaches to life.

Some in the body of Christ fear that if we set down the right-and-wrong descriptions of the faith, we will devolve into soft-selling the gospel. However, holiness is not for sale. Any church that spends its energy focusing on the life of Jesus will lead people toward Christlikeness, which is the greatest vision and embodiment of holiness this world has ever seen. Beyond that, a centered Christianity erases judgmental attitudes and instead welcomes the secular population into a conversation they are wanting to have—the life of Jesus the Christ. That being true, another season of Jesus Stories is quickly approaching. While our past has been about protecting borders, our future will be centered on the life and times of Christ. May we become as enthralled with the life stories of Jesus as was the first church.

Birthing Faith

The first steps an unbeliever takes toward Christ is as monumental as a toddler's first step. It changes everything. So, how does first faith birth in the human heart? Paul obviously spent time pondering this question, which inspired his words in Romans 10:17: "So then faith comes by hearing, and hearing by the word of God." In our day, we read this verse a bit differently than the first church did. We assume that Paul was saying that faith births from the scriptures. And while that is a wonderful thought, we know that was not what Paul meant, because it would be another 310 years before the canon of scriptures would be collated and codified by Athanasius.[21] Paul's audience would have heard the phrase "word of God" to mean the living Word—the person of Jesus. We see this clearly in John 1:14: "So the Word became human and made his home among us." So, Jesus is the Word that John was writing about. Thus, talking about the Jesus Stories was perceived by the apostles as what would birth faith in the human heart. We might assume that our teaching outlines from scripture are inspiring faith, but Paul would point us back to retelling the stories from the life and times of Jesus as the richer, faith-inspiring material.

Paul was so affected by the preeminence of the Jesus Stories that he wrote in Romans 1:16, "I am not ashamed of the Gospel of Christ. It is the power of God to salvation for everyone who believes, for the Jew and also the Greek." The gospel of Christ is not a modernist constructed paragraph that explains an overview

---

21. "No church or council created the canon, but the churches and councils gradually accepted the list of books recognized by believers everywhere as inspired. It was actually not until 367 AD that the church father Athanasius first provided the complete listing of the 66 books belonging to the canon." www.biblica.com/resources/bible-faqs/how-were-the-books-of-the-bible-chosen.

of Christianity, nor is it a collation of the major affirmations of scripture like the Apostles' Creed. It is, however, the actual and various Jesus Stories reported by the four Gospel writers. This is the unique content that operates in great power and births faith in the heart of the sinner. The reason Jesus Stories are so powerful is that Jesus himself accompanies the retelling of his stories. And he will keep that story and his presence stirring in an unbeliever's heart long after the retelling event is over. We might be only telling a story, but Jesus is introducing himself. This is how faith is birthed. Once we know how the Jesus Stories breathe great power into secular conversations, we begin to relax in our evangelism moments.

Empowered for the Task

Bringing someone to the Savior is no small task, but the heavy lifting is not actually on our shoulders. Our role in the partnership is quite small. Nonetheless, we are called to enter into that partnership and succeed in that call. Paul said, "I have a great sense of obligation to people in both the civilized world, and the rest of the world; to the educated and the uneducated alike" (Rom. 1:14, NLT). We have the same obligation as did the apostles and the first church. However, due to increasing ineffectiveness over the years, we have become discouraged and drifted from the obligation. When we don't know how to do something effectively, we stop trying. That is human nature. However, to win back the Jesus Stories as our content for evangelism enables us to rise again to the challenge of the Great Commission.

We have been uniquely impressed and empowered by the Spirit to be highly effective at witnessing to the life and times of

Jesus—far more than most realize. Paul gave a huge insight about this in 2 Corinthians 6:2: "On the day of salvation I helped you. Indeed, the right time is now. Today is the day of salvation." If we are living in the day of salvation, what was the previous day? And what changed? These are valid questions. We are so accustomed to living in this unique moment of human history that we have become dulled to what a special privilege it is. There were significant changes that occurred the day Jesus rose. Not only did he become the sacrificial lamb to afford the price of salvation, but something profound shifted in the heavenlies to empower this new day of salvation.

Three of the four Gospels recorded that when Jesus died the veil in the temple was torn in two—the very veil that separated Holy of Holies from the rest of the temple. The Shekinah flame dwelt in that space, which represented the physical presence of God on the earth. When the curtain was torn, it was revealed that the flame of God's presence was no longer burning in the Holy of Holies. Then, fifty days later, in Acts 2:4, the Shekinah flame returned, but rather than in a temple it returned on the heads of 120 Christ followers in the upper room. These two events are theologically paired. But what does it mean? Previously, God's presence had resided on the earth in the temple in Jerusalem, as evidenced by his Shekinah flame. But after Acts 2, God altered the manner by which he dwelt on the earth. In other words, he moved into the human bodies of the redeemed as evidenced by his new flame. He made his people into mobile temples and empowered them with his very presence. Such an indwelling had never been experienced before by humans.

Even the prophets in the Old Testament had the Spirit come upon them as they prophesied, but it would dissipate once they were done. After the day of Pentecost, the Spirit of God moved into the very bodies of his people. This is what the day of salvation means to us in real time: the Spirit of God resides inside of us to empower us for the great missional task. We need to own this fact, that God chose to rewire how he would pour himself on the earth.

The people of God have been uniquely impressed and empowered by the Spirit in this chapter of human history. It was not like this prior to Jesus' coming, and we know from John 9:4 that this day of salvation will not last forever. In fact, Ezekiel 43:4 reveals that the presence of God will again move into the New Temple one day, but for now we have an unusual ability and power for evangelism because the very Spirit of God is living within us.

Jesus augmented the meaning of the day of salvation by offering a great promise to the Church in Acts 1:8: "But you will receive power when the Holy Spirit comes upon you; and you will be my witnesses"(NIV). I have already clarified in an earlier section that this was not a charge to engage in witnessing, but rather to be a witness about the life and times of Jesus, to tell the many stories about Jesus. Once we get that straight, we understand the divine strategy for evangelism. We can partner with the divine in our gospel vocation and expect power to flow from our words when we are talking with secular people. Even in pressure-filled moments, we should anticipate help bubbling up from within us. Luke 12:11–12 captures Jesus saying, "When you are brought to trial before rulers and authorities, don't worry about what to say, for the Holy Spirit will teach you at that time what needs to be said." Of course, Jesus assumed the forthcoming empowerments of the day of salvation when he spoke this, but it is a promise of prophetic anointing for each of us in this day.

This changes things. We are never just telling Jesus Stories. The Jesus Stories will be flooding out of us, being driven along by the Holy Spirit. No wonder Jesus gains so much ground in people's lives when we just tell the stories that the Spirit brings to our minds. I will say it again. We have been uniquely impresenced and empowered by the Spirit to be effective in witnessing about the life and times of Jesus the Christ.

Practical Approaches

Evangelism is far easier when you have the Jesus Stories stirring around in your soul. Once we shake off the Reformation-era evangelism outlines and talking points, and endeavor to embrace the first church's approach, we are well on our way.

Most Christians who have begun building their own faith on the Jesus Stories find evangelism to be rather easy. The Jesus Stories flow out of them so naturally that it is not until later that it dawns on them they were actually witnessing to the life of Christ. And that is all witnessing is. So, what you don't need is an evangelistic outline right now.

What you do need is to read yourself full of Jesus' life stories, trust the Spirit to bring those stories out in natural ways, and get yourself to a place in which secular people are present. Over time, interesting and spiritual conversations will naturally emerge. Jesus and his first followers looked for tables. You might do the same.

Go Preach the Gospel—
the Way I Did

Each of the Great Commission statements highlights a different directive from Jesus. We have already considered Luke's version in an earlier chapter, but let us now consider Peter's Great Commission remembrance, which was penned by young John Mark.[1] Mark 16:15 records: "Go into all the world and preach the gospel to all creation" (NIV). Now, look closely at the spiritual content Jesus directed to be preached: "the gospel."

Once again, we have done something with these words that align with the reductions of modernism. We have turned "the gospel" into a holistic overview of the important points from the life of Christ. And yet, what I believe Jesus intended was for us to tell his gospel stories and teachings—the way he did it. Our present practice of speaking through the entire scriptures has been edifying, to be sure, but it is not same thing Jesus asked for. I propose there is value in focusing on the exact preaching material Jesus used and directed us to retell.

This past year the radio on my Jeep stopped working, so I had a new one installed. However, it did not sound as good as the stock sound system had, so I took it back to the installer. They

---

1. Green, *Evangelism in the Early Church*, 319.

explained that the old deck only served the mid-ranges of sound, and my speakers were only designed for those mid-ranges too. In other words, this new deck was sending more ranges of sound than the old speakers could handle. The result was barrel-like reverberation. So, I paid a bit extra to have them install a subwoofer, and *oh my goodness*, what a difference. I had no idea a Jeep could sound like a concert hall.

Something similar has been happening in Christian presentations. Our teaching-based approaches are serving the tones that only Judeo populations can appreciate. If we are going to speak in a way that secular people can appreciate, we will need to reconsider the historic *kerygma*. With over 60 percent of the US population now holding to a secular worldview, recovering Christ's version of story-form preaching is rather urgent. What is the future of Christianity if the majority of the population cannot adequately process the spiritual content we are delivering? But, when we preach the Jesus-Stories and the gospel narratives, *oh my goodness*, what a difference.

Teaching versus Preaching

Over the past few decades, a new tension has arisen for church leaders: preaching versus teaching.[2] Truth be told, our version of speaking isn't actually preaching at all. It is teaching. What we call preaching is usually just teaching but with a bit more verve and volume. Actual Apostolic-era preaching hasn't been regularly practiced by the church for centuries. The New Testament uses two different words to explain Christian speaking. One term used

2. Harold Westing, *Celebrate Your Church's Uniqueness* (Grand Rapids, MI: Kregel, 1993), 228.

is *didache*, from which we derive the understanding of teaching. The other term is *kerygma*, from which we derive the understanding of preaching. Sadly, in our day we have been so far removed from the practice of *kerygma* that we don't know what we don't know. Theologian C. H. Dodd states, "There is a careful distinction between preaching (kerygma) and teaching (didache) in the Early Church."[3]

For an example of kerygmatic preaching from the Apostolic era, one has to look no further than the book of Mark. The very earliest Christian community met in the upper room of a particular house in Jerusalem, owned by the mother of John Mark.[4] Apostolic father Papias reports that it was in this upper room where pastor Peter came to preach, and young John Mark, who was sixteen years of age and was literate, wrote down on papyrus what he heard.[5] So what did Peter's preaching sound like? According to Mark's writings, he merely retold the stories about Jesus and the stories that Jesus told; apostolic preaching content was focused on the Jesus Stories. It was not just Peter who modeled this. On no fewer than nine occasions Paul stated that when he preached, he "preached Christ."[6] Similarly, the Gospels of Matthew, Luke, and John followed Mark's form of retelling the Jesus Stories, which reveals their preaching approaches as well. Then, as stated in chapter 1, the after-gospel portions of the New Testament (Acts through Revelation) reveal ninety-four different times when preaching, teaching, proclaiming, and testifying were directly connected to

3.   Richard Niebuhr and Daniel Williams, *The Ministry in Historical Perspectives* (Eugene, OR: Wipf and Stock, 2001), 15.
4.   Green, *Evangelism in the Early Church*, 319.
5.   Green, *Evangelism in the Early Church*, 98.
6.   Romans 15:20; 1 Corinthians 1:17, 23; 9:18; 2 Corinthians 2:12; 4:5; Ephesians 3:8; Philippians 1:15; Colossians 1:28.

the Jesus narratives (see appendix A). Flatly stated, retelling the life and times of Jesus was their preaching content, and story form was their method of delivery. That makes sense because Jesus did that too.

This simplicity of Jesus-Story preaching has been mostly lost on us in this modernist era, though many have fought for its recovery. American theologian Richard Neibuhr, quoting C. H. Dodd, says that preaching is the proclamation of the good news of the saving action in the life, death, and resurrection of Christ.[7] Twentieth-century theologian Karl Barth believed that preaching should be based on the life of Christ.[8] Harvey Cox laments that we have departed today from the preaching of the apostles. They followed a practice of presenting something that happened in the life of Jesus and something yet to happen: his coming again with power.[9] Michael Green's research reveals that the early preachers of the gospel had one subject and one only: Jesus.[10] In our day we understand teaching quite well, but we are profoundly underpracticed in the use of Jesus-Story preaching. This is a problem because secular people are not likely to appreciate *didache* presentations as much as kerygmatic proclamation. There is a reason the church has lost its evangelistic voice.

The *Kerygma*'s Demise

In Jesus' day meals dominated the Roman nightlife. These evenings concluded with a symposium, which created an opportunity for entertainers and speakers to flourish. This gave rise to

7.   Niebuhr and Williams, *The Ministry in Historical Perspectives*, 16.
8.   Avery Dulles, *Models of the Church* (New York: Doubleday, 2002), 174.
9.   Cox, *The Secular City,* 122.
10.   Green, *Evangelism in the Early Church*, 80.

the philosophical art of rhetoric, which was a form of persuasive speech akin to the Ted Talks of today. These cultural meals affected Judaism, including their speaking forms. Dennis E. Smith states that Judaism during the Roman occupation was highly Hellenized, not only among those Jews, but also in pockets of Hebrew and Aramaic conservatism.[11] This affected their religious practices, including their readings. But, when Jesus came, he shifted the speaking paradigm of his day.[12] We see this shift in several Gospel accounts, in which he taught as one having authority, not as the scribes.[13] Jesus' disciples preached in the same fashion as their rabbi, which gave them similar authority to preach with power, cast out demons, and heal the sick. Preaching with power and functioning with power defined the first church throughout the book of Acts and the New Testament. Potent preaching is what drove the rebuke of the religious leaders in Acts 5:28 who charged the apostles for spreading the gospel message throughout the entire city after being warned not to talk about Jesus. As noted earlier, Paul was asked to speak in rhetoric form, and he said no. When he preached, he preferred to preach Jesus crucified.

Nonetheless, there came a time when the patterns of the age undercut the story-form method Jesus had left with the church. Alan Hirsch states that preaching was quickly affected by rhetoric and that preachers were leaning into the persuasive arts of the Greek and Roman techniques.[14] Christian historian James White reports the same, that the preachers of the Patristic period bor-

11. Dennis E. Smith, *From Symposium to Eucharist: The Banquet in the Early Christian World* (Minneapolis: Fortress, 2003), Kindle loc. 296.

12. Andrew Davies, "A New Teaching Without Authority: Preaching the Bible in Postmodernity," *Journal of the European Pentecostal Theological Association 27, no. 2* (2007): 164.

13. Matthew 7:29; Mark 1:22; Luke 4:22.

14. Frost and Hirsch, *The Shaping of Things to Come*, 151.

rowed from pagan culture the rhetoric skills that had been formed over centuries, and that Christians had come to appreciate the great tradition of persuasive public speaking.[15] By the time we get to Augustine and Chrysostom we see that rhetoric-form speaking was assumed. In fact, Chrysostom garnered the nickname Golden Mouth for his persuasive abilities.[16]

Today we are far removed from the kerygmatic speaking form. Our version of church that was developed by theological professors during the Reformation had never been practiced before. It was modeled around the classroom and the lecturing professor, which assumed a teaching-based delivery of information. As people were breaking away from Catholicism and its sacred-space sociologies, they needed a different-looking form of church. They certainly found that with the classroom design: people seated facing forward, quietly listening to the professor-like pastor up front. This shift did nothing to recover story-form speaking that Jesus used. In fact, it launched a completely different speaking approach based on bullet points and sequential outlines.

In the 1800s, a significant contrast occurred with the Great Awakening, which thunderously burst upon the church with preaching forms based on a Word from God. It was different, and it was needed to remind everyone that Christianity was not cerebral, but rather hearty and relational. Early in the twentieth century, a pendulum swing occurred among liberal churches with the Topical Preaching movement. This speaking form moved away from the word from God, and instead focused on the felt needs of the congregation.[17] Then the Church Growth movement of the

---

15.   James White, *A Brief History of Christian Worship* (Nashville: Abingdon, 1993), 69.

16.   White, *A Brief History of Christian Worship*, 70.

17.   White, *A Brief History of Christian Worship*, 171.

late twentieth century altered preaching again by directing Christian speakers to develop their stage abilities to appeal to wider and larger gatherings. Ultimately, this gave rise to the rock-star pastors we see in many pulpits today. In recent decades we have watched the emergence of verse-by-verse teaching, which some denominations argue is the only valid form of preaching.[18]

However, thick teaching and stage-heavy Christian presentations are losing effectiveness in this post-Christian era. A generation has arrived that is no longer interested in an upfront person talking to them in one-way communication and telling them how to live. Preaching pastor Fred Craddock refers to the Reformation's preaching styles as setting up the congregation to be like javelin catchers. The only participation is for the audience to "get the point."[19] Mike Graves uses a different metaphor to explain popular Christian teaching as watching a chef prepare a meal but never getting to taste it.[20] Once again, the audience's participation is limited and unsatisfactory. We now have a generation who has come along and said, "Enough." We are now facing a secular community who has made it abundantly clear that it is not interested in stage lectures.

Truth be told, this form of speaking has been ineffective at making people into functional disciples of Jesus for a long time now. While it has been good at making good church people, it has not been effective at making fiery Christ followers. Christian philosopher Søren Kierkegaard saw this coming when he published the parable called "The Domestic Goose." Each Sunday these geese waddled down to their goose church to hear the goose

---

18. Ed Stetzer, *Planting New Churches in a Postmodern Age* (Nashville: B&H, 2003), 277.
19. Graves, *Table Talk*, 98.
20. Graves, *Table Talk*, 99.

preacher say, "We are geese and geese are meant to fly." Then after a few amens, the geese would leave church and waddle back home.[21] What a painfully honest depiction of the limitations of Christian teaching as we are presently practicing it. What was intended to be a revelation of the God-man, Jesus Christ, in an offensive form of preaching has now devolved into a weekly routine with placid, predictable results.[22] But such is to be expected when our content and form of delivery has become buried by strata after strata of speaking forms that are very different from the Jesus Stories template of the first century.

Jesus Stories and the Preacher

Apostolic preaching was potent. But it began by the speakers embracing the Jesus Stories into their souls and then letting those stories flow out with power and authority. Just as Jesus spoke with such surprising authority that demons fled, so his disciples spoke. Anyone who uses the Jesus Stories finds an unusual anointing coming on them. Michael Green states, "The Kerygma was no dull monochrome, but rather a many splendored thing."[23] The story-based preaching Jesus instilled in his disciples was potent and authoritative. Paul used an interesting word to create confidence in preaching—*plerophoria*—where preachers were so full of the Spirit of God and so persuaded of the truth of their message that it overflowed from them.[24] Rex Miller asks, "Why were Jesus' words so powerful? Because they contain the living essence of Je-

21. Graves, *Table Talk*, 93.
22. Dietrich Bonhoeffer, *Christ the Center* (New York: HarperOne, 1978), 46.
23. Green, *Evangelism in the Early Church*, 383.
24. Green, *Evangelism in the Early Church*, 262.

sus' presence."[25] Jesus' words are supposed to have a deep impact on us, and when our personal salvation is built on the Jesus Stories, we can preach a house on fire.

Preaching has had a unique impact on our nation. Woodrow Wilson once said that one of the great proofs of the divinity of the gospel is the preaching it has survived.[26] This is both a funny and a sad commentary on the potential dilutions of preaching. However, early Americana reveals a preaching that was anything but diluted and impotent. French philosopher Alexis de Tocqueville came to America in 1831 to study our nation. His report read,

> I sought for the key to the greatness and genius of America in her harbors; in her fertile fields and boundless forests; in her rich mines and vast world commerce; in her public school system and institutions of learning. I sought for it in her democratic congress and in her matchless Constitution. Not until I went into the churches of America and heard her pulpits aflame with righteousness did I understand the secret of her genius and power. America is great because America is good, and if America ever ceases to be good, America will cease to be great.[27]

Three decades later, nineteenth-century preacher William Lloyd Garrison preached with such fire that President Lincoln shuddered at what God would do if slavery continued in our land.[28] Our nation has been deeply affected by preaching throughout our history.

---

25. Miller, *The Millennium Matrix*, 24.

26. Mario Murillo, "A New Kind of Christian Leader," Mario Murillo Ministries, March 9, 2020, https://mariomurillo.org/2020/03/09/a-new-kind-of-christian-leader/.

27. Dutch Sheets, "Give Him Fifteen," July 28, 2021, https://www.givehim15.com/.

28. Curtis Chang, *Engaging Unbelief: The Captivating Strategy from Augustine to Aquinas* (Eugene, OR: Wipf and Stock, 2000), 171.

But we are living in a new day, and we must learn a version of preaching that holds power in these times. So, how does a preacher learn to flow with the Spirit and power? Raymond Lull would answer that question by asking a developing preacher if he or she was willing to suffer for the gospel.[29] How would you like to hear that question in an ordination interview? British evangelist G. Campbell Morgan once listened to a young pastor speak. Afterward, he commented that the young man was a very good preacher, and when he suffered, he would be a great preacher.[30] There is a special bond between suffering and power in preaching. This might shed new light on the challenges and setbacks you have faced throughout your ministry. It certainly causes much of my life to make more sense. Jesus suffered rejection of the highest order but preached with power. The disciples suffered abandonment and arrest just like their master but preached with power. A similar pattern of sacrifice will work its wonder in every minister of the gospel who will embrace it. Christlikeness applies to more than our Christian faith. It applies to our preaching as well. We suffer with him, we preach his stories, and we preach to his kind of people. If you are called to preach, a measure of suffering is assumed.

Short, Simple, and Prophetic

I noted earlier that one of the best examples of Apostolic-era preaching is the book of Mark. It appears that pastor Peter's preaching was quite short. When reading Mark, you can imagine Peter conclud-

29. Timothy Tennent, *How God Saves the World: A Short History of Global Christianity* (Franklin, TN: Seedbed, 2016), 36–37.
30. Leith Anderson, *A Church for the 21st Century* (Minneapolis: Bethany House, 1992), 203.

ing each Jesus Story with a prayer and then dismissing those gathered until next week when a new Jesus Story would be preached. Except for Paul preaching so long that Eutychus drifted to sleep and fell out of an upper window (Acts 20:9), there is nothing to suggest that the preaching at these agape churches were long. Jesus Stories and sermons were provably short. Why would we assume anything different for his disciples? Interestingly, the disciples never once asked Jesus to teach them to preach.[31] They asked him to teach them to pray, to cast out demons, and how to have more faith. But they never asked him how to preach. Jesus' preaching was obviously so simple, both in structure and length, that the disciples felt they could replicate it without extra training from the Master. According to Richard Niebuhr, Luther was not in favor of overlong sermons either. His preaching, like his table talk, was quite simple.[32]

One of my graduate students at the Dinner Church School of Leadership was attempting to preach one of his first-ever kerygmatic sermons. When he was done, he asked his congregation for feedback, and one of the newer ladies in the crowd said, "Geesh . . . even I could do that!" Everyone laughed, but the pastor wisely said, "And isn't that the point? So, when are you going to preach a Jesus Story?" I find that response to be brilliant. The gospel should be simple enough that anyone can do it. This sheds new light on Paul's instructions to Timothy: "Preach the word; be ready in season and out of season" (2 Tim. 4:2 NIV). Such readiness is possible if preaching is retelling the simple stories of Jesus. Similarly, Peter said, "Always be prepared to give an answer to everyone who asks you to give a reason for the hope that you have" (1 Pet. 3:15 NIV).

---

31.   Jim Cymbala, "We Got to Change Up The Game" (lecture to pastors at General Council of the Assemblies of God, Orlando, FL, August 6, 2014).

32.   Niebuhr and Williams, *The Ministry in Historical Perspectives*, 134.

Once again, this level of readiness is realistic when we assume that the simple stories of Jesus will be the basis of the explanation. If Jesus is really good at his job, telling his stories in short and simple ways should be enough, right?

Today, we have turned preaching into a complex performance. And yet we need to be careful about the consumerism it creates, especially with our preaching forms being so different from the simple stories Jesus told and the first church repeated.[33] While I love hearing longer teaching-based sermons, I have to acknowledge these are constructs that were developed centuries after the life and times of Christ. Truth be told, the most effective preaching is simple and easy to remember.[34] Some believe that the book of Mark has actually been used through the eras to deprofessionalize preaching and seize it back for the people.[35] Andrew Davies states that maybe preaching could survive as the church's primary means of communication if a generation of preachers was prepared to follow the example of Christ.[36]

Some years ago, I overheard a woman talking to a friend at a gym about a dinner she had started attending in the Magnusson neighborhood of Seattle. I immediately recognized it as one of our dinner church sites, so I listened closely to what followed. She had originally attended because she was tasked with opening the community center for that dinner church, but they invited her to stay and eat with them. After a few weeks of opening the door for these people and eating with them, she asked for a permanent assignment with the community center so she could go every week. And then

33.   Dan Kimball, *Emerging Worship: Creating Worship Gatherings for New Generations* (Grand Rapids, MI: Zondervan, 2004), 35.

34.   Stetzer, *Planting New Churches in a Postmodern Age*, 280.

35.   Davies, "A New Teaching Without Authority," 171.

36.   Davies, "A New Teaching Without Authority," 171.

66

she told her friend this: "I have never understood Christianity, or been interested throughout my life. But after eating and hearing their speakers tell stories from the life of Christ, I have found it to be so interesting. I find myself thinking about that story all week long." Then her friend said, "I have known you for years and never saw you as someone who would be intrigued by Christianity." I was so thankful I got to overhear that conversation; I know the Lord arranged that for me to hear. The power of one of these 468 Jesus Stories is surprising, even among lifelong secular people.

Lesslie Newbigin points out that wherever the gospel has been preached, new ideologies have appeared: secular humanism, nationalism, Marxism—movements that offer a vision of a new age that is freed from all ills.[37] We are watching these appearances in our land in real time. These are serious days we are living in. We need to know how to speak with power. In Romans 1:16 Paul said he was not ashamed of the gospel stories, because they are the power of God to bring salvation to everyone—Jews and Gentiles. One of our seminary presidents was on a flight and ended up sitting next to a Jewish rabbi. After a long conversation about several spiritual leadership issues, the rabbi turned and said, "Your pastors need to remember that when they speak, they speak for God!"[38] What the world needs during these pluralistic times is preaching that flows from the authoritative life of Jesus, rather than teaching outlines crafted by human rationales. Charles Spurgeon once said that choosing what to preach is like a doctor choosing medicine for a patient.[39] These are sobering decisions. Sick people and flat-lined

---

37. Newbiggin, *The Gospel in a Pluralist Society*, 122.
38. Byron Klaus, (lecture to master's class, Manchester, UK, February 2012).
39. Kimball, *Emerging Worship*, 105.

societies hang in the balance. We would do well to consider versions of preaching that are less modernistic and more Christ-centric.

Preaching to the Poor

Who is your favorite preacher? If he or she is never speaking to the poor, that person is not the same kind of preacher as Jesus.[40] The day Jesus showed up in the synagogue in his hometown of Nazareth and read from the scroll of Isaiah of his ministry mandate, he promised that he would be preaching to the poor.[41] Jesus' preaching cannot be separated from preaching to the poor, no matter how much we may feel the need to separate it. At Jesus' last supper, he carried over the historic pattern of gathering the liminal and family-less people at the Passovers, and he embedded it into the New Passovers going forward. In so doing he was formalizing his new version of preaching—one that assumed an impoverished audience would be present.

Leonard Sweet reports that some of the greatest awakenings in Christian history occurred when preachers escaped from their pulpit prisons and started preaching in the streets and fields.[42] A deeper study by author Paul Engle reveals eight characteristics of revival movements over the centuries. One of them is a restoration of preaching to the poor.[43] There is not a lot of preaching to the poor in our day, which presents us with a glaring preaching problem. The missiological situation has so changed in post-

40. "Benjamin Corey," Facebook, March 6, 2016.
41. Isaiah 61:1.
42. Leonard Sweet, *Aqua Church 2.0* (Colorado Springs: David C. Cook, 1999), 25.
43. Paul Engle and Gary McIntosh, *Evaluating the Church Growth Movement: 5 Views* (Grand Rapids, MI: Zondervan, 2004), 219–20.

Christian America that we desperately need to escape our pulpit prisons again.

London pastor Charles Spurgeon's preaching model was this: preach the gospel and meet the needs of the city, especially the poor.[44] In recent decades many in the church have realized that social action prepares the way for the preaching of the cross, but it is also justified for its own sake and not merely as a lever for evangelism.[45] English theologian John Stott speaks of evangelism and social action as being equal partners of the Christian mission.[46] Ministry to the poor should be home turf for preachers and preaching, but that is not always the case. However, it is home turf for dinner churches past and present. At these Jesus tables the rich, the poor, the saints, the sinners, the sacred, and the profane are all gathered to hear the preaching of the gospel. Mike Graves says, "There is something different about preaching when it happens at a table."[47] Preaching to rooms full of secular sinners will change any preacher. But be warned, anyone who becomes effective at preaching to the poor and reaching the secular lost will earn criticisms from the veterans of the church.[48] Sad but true.

Preaching to Lost Hearts

Though most preaching today is done in sanctuaries where most of the crowd is already saved, speaking to the lost is Christianity's historic sweet spot. Karl Barth once said, "Christian leaders ought

---

44. Darrin Patrick and Matt Carter, *For the City: Proclaiming and Living Out the Gospel* (Grand Rapids, MI: Zondervan, 2010), 23.
45. Michael Griffiths, *Shaking the Sleeping Beauty: Arousing the Church to Its Mission* (Leicester, UK: 1980), 106.
46. Griffiths, *Shaking the Sleeping Beauty*, 106.
47. Graves, *Table Talk*, 104.
48. Brian McLaren, *A New Kind of Christian* (San Francisco: Jossey-Bass, 2001),17.

to preach with a Bible in one hand, and newspaper in the other."[49] In other words, preaching is supposed to be connected to market-place issues. American evangelist Ed Silvoso points out that Jesus' work in his father's carpentry business made him a businessman much longer than he was a preacher.[50] We might want to meditate on the implications of that a bit. The first recorded statement of preaching was to a throng in the streets after Pentecost. The mar-ketplace and the street are theology's natural home.[51] This makes a significant case for dinner churches because they meet and preach in marketplace environments. Even if a pastor has been trained for insider preaching, that pastor will find him- or herself pivot-ing to street-worthy relevance fast once he or she is preaching to rooms full of lost people.

Antioch was a prominent place in scripture; it was there that the gospel was first preached to people who had no connection to Judaism.[52] It was the frontlines of evangelism. As it turns out, the first church's preaching on Jesus Stories was effective among the Gentile and pagan peoples. Soong-Chan Rah says the church grew from 120 in an upper room to 34 million in the first three centuries among Greco-Roman peoples.[53] In our day, the rate of conversion to Christ worldwide is approximately 100,000 per day, and most are in the two-thirds world where they must preach in the face of entrenched faiths like Animism, Buddhism, Hindu-ism, and Islam.[54] Again, the church can be good at preaching to

---

49.   Bobby Ross, February 27, 2021, http:christianchronicle.org.
50.   Neil Johnson, 169.
51.   Earl Creps, *Off-Roads Disciplines* (San Francisco: Jossey-Bass, 2006), 132.
52.   Green, *Evangelism in the Early Church*, 162.
53.   Soong-Chan Rah, *The Next Evangelicalism: Freeing the Church from Western Cultural Captivity* (Downers Grove, IL: InterVarsity, 2009), 105.
54.   Green, *Evangelism in the Early Church*, 22.

under-gospeled people, especially if we focus on the Jesus Stories like the first church did.

What the *Kerygma* Is Not

While teaching is about edifying the saints, first-century preaching was about compelling lost people to the Savior by retelling the Jesus Stories. This has become a lost art in this day of the church-man. While some are beginning to see what kerygmatic preaching looks like, we must also see that isn't a doctrinal treatise, a scriptural sequential lesson, or a spiritual lecture. The Jesus Stories are not as directive as the other preaching forms that have been practiced over the centuries. Academic Martha Leypoldt states that we should never, ever lecture . . . unless there is no other way to help a person learn.[55]

Story-form preaching does not parse spiritual material in the ways that teachings and lectures would. Herein lies our challenge. Most Christian speakers today have been trained in apologetics, systemic theology, exegesis, hermeneutics, and etymological word studies as the ingredients of their teachings. These things lead to what Leonard Sweet refers to as "versitis," which means mining the book for minutiae rather than stories. Sadly, this inevitably leads to the greatest story never half-told rather than the greatest story ever told.[56] Modernism and its rational constructs have not been kind to the art of preaching.

Perhaps in the next era of the church, we will set down the speaking forms that have proved to be ineffective with the people we are called to reach. I hope Ed Stetzer is right when he says

---

55. Robert Anderson, *Circles of Influence* (Chicago: Moody Press, 1991), 210.
56. Sweet, *Tablet to Table*. 28.

that narrative preaching will increase throughout the future of the church.[57] That will be a welcomed sight for the *kerygma*.

One of our dinner churches is in the Ballard neighborhood of Seattle, which is a place where two worlds collide. One population works at Amazon and can afford $4,000 per month for their high-rise apartments; the other population are the homeless, the longshoremen and ship welders who work on the waterfront, and the fishermen. It is the latter group that filled our dinner church on Tuesday nights. These are tough people. If you are willing to be flown to the Bering Sea to live and work on a processor ship for twelve weeks at a time or be thrown into the belly of a ship with a welder in your hand for twelve-hour shifts, you are a special kind of person. It was in that room that Brian, one of our dinner church pastors, had just finished preaching. As he was praying over everyone, he felt something brushing up against his leg. When he glanced down, he saw one of these men on his knees weeping, and his forehead was bumping against Brian's leg. Soon Brian heard something on the other side, and when he glanced it was another of these tough men kneeling on that side. Then a third man came and knelt behind him. When Brian finished praying, he said he did not know what else to do, so he got down on his knees and felt great compassion come over him, and he began to weep as well. The room remained completely quiet and we watched what was happening up front, and then others began to come forward, putting their arms around each other and checking that everyone was OK. It turned into a deeply spiritual altar moment among the toughest people in our city. When Brian told my wife and me about this, we asked him which Jesus Story he had preached. He looked at us blankly and said, "I don't remember." We broke out

---

57.   Stetzer, 279.

laughing. In fairness to him, he had preached several other times since that evening. Here's my point: the Jesus Stories that seem so simple and elemental to the average churchgoer are so unspeakably powerful to lost hearts, even the rugged ones.

Practical Approaches

Teaching is a practiced skill in our traditional churches, something only the seminary trained professional's attempt. This is not the case with the *kerygma*. It is simple enough that lay pastors and maturing Christians can do it well, and the Gospel needs them to do it. The simple outline I give to a newly developing Seattle pastors is this:

- Read some Jesus Stories to yourself until one flares up in your soul.
- Read that story to the room.
- Retell that story in your own words.
- Highlight one point from the story that is stirring in you.
- Reveal how that story has become meaningful to you in your life.
- Pray a generous prayer over everyone with whatever flows out of your soul.

That's it. But don't confuse simplicity with frailty. Jesus Stories flowing from humble people is a huge thing. When it comes to the *kerygma*, the power of the presentation is not in the winsome speech of the speaker. It is how Jesus reveals himself to the sinner's heart from his own stories. You will be long done preaching, but that story will still be pulsating in the souls of your hearers for weeks.

Appendix C is an overview of the 468 Jesus Story titles. Perhaps reading over these titles will resonate as a starting point for a preaching selection. A more detailed resource on Jesus Story sermon formation has been created by the American Bible Society and can be found in appendix B. I fully recommend it as an important outline for thought.

Make Disciples—Teach Them What I Told You

T he church today has adopted a definition of discipleship that infuses the full scriptures, Genesis to Revelation, into the minds of the students. But that was not exactly what Jesus asked for. In Matthew's recollection of the Great Commission Jesus said, "Go and make disciples, teaching them to obey *what I taught you*" (Matt. 28:19–20, emphasis mine). What was that? What was the teaching content Jesus directed his disciples to use? He told us to use his words, his teachings, his stories, and the chronicles of his life events. He did not leave us with a scripture reading plan, or Bible bases, or a series of discipleship classes, or any other modernist construct of spirituality drawn from the sixty-six books of the Bible. What he did leave us was his life stories and teachings for us to prioritize in disciple-making—468 gospel narratives, to be exact. (See appendix C for a list.)

Here is a provoking question: What if we made disciples from the material that Jesus left behind for us to use? Now, don't get me wrong; I believe the Bible is inspired and helpful and useful for Christian leadership. But I am simply noting that Jesus told us to do something different than studying the scriptures and calling it disciple-making.

Discipleship by a Different Name

The word *discipleship* is never mentioned in the Bible. We are told merely to make disciples.[1] However, our present concepts have us focusing on the process of discipleship more than the outcomes in the life of the disciple, a variance that is not proving very successful. What passes for discipleship today produces believers who are lacking spiritual stamina. Our faith is a greenhouse faith that is only capable of thriving in controlled environments.[2] Ouch! J. R. Briggs, a content creator and presenter for Fresh Expressions, as well as an author, speaker, and church consultant, reports that only 25 percent of American Christians meet the minimal scriptural definition of discipleship.[3]

One pastor tells of a time when he was asking his church to engage in a missional activity. After much effort, only one-third of his church backed the initiative. The pastors reported, "I was really shaken up. It made me deeply reflect on the impact of my own pastoral leadership. I came to the horrifying conclusion that we had built our church on sand and not discipleship."[4] While some feel their Sunday morning teachings are sufficient for disciple-making, most are realizing that their people are being formed to gather and listen, but are increasingly unwilling for even minor missional engagements.

American theologian Dallas Willard says that discipleship is the elephant in the room of the local church.[5] Something has gone wrong in the way we are training the workforce of the body

---

1. Anderson, *Circles of Influence*, 336.
2. Lawless and Greenway, *The Great Commission Resurgence*, 232.
3. J. R. Briggs, (Lecture, Fresh Expressions National Gathering, Alexandria, VA, April 9, 2016).
4. Alan Hirsch, *The Forgotten Ways* (Grand Rapids, MI: Brazos, 2006), 40–42.
5. Winfield Bevens, (Lecture, Fresh Expressions National Gathering, Alexandria, VA, April 8, 2016).

of Christ. They are incapable of shouldering the necessary tasks for the inbreaking kingdom of God. We must disrupt these consumer ideas with a better vision of following Jesus. In the words of Anglican bishop Graham Cray, "A consumer lifestyle can't be overturned by criticism, it can only be outclassed by the Christlike lifestyle."[6]

Discipleship by a different name is Christlikeness. Quite frankly, I think the term *Christlikeness* points us down a different road than the term *discipleship* in these days. *Discipleship* can assume all kinds of things from scripture and church history. *Christlikeness* is more focused. It assumes we are starting with Jesus' stories, which leads to his actual behaviors, actions, words, and activities. Present-day discipleship models are commonly values-based and principles-focused teaching from the full scriptures. While that is not a bad thing, it is not the same thing that Jesus asked of us; he proposed a behavior-based version of disciple-making drawn from his own life and words. I am not suggesting a works-based salvation, but I am suggesting a version of disciple formation that flows from an adherence to Christ-centric behaviors. The church in the West faces a choice: continue with values-based discipleship or pivot to behavior-based Christlikeness. And the two are not the same.

Alan Hirsch offers the critique that reading the Gospels through the Epistles creates a disturbing distortion; the Gospels are not taken as a serious prescriptive for life, mission, and discipleship.[7] It is possible to dilute the unique power of the Jesus Stories in discipleship by promoting all scripture as equal. While scriptural texts create good students, Jesus Stories create followers

---

6. Graham Cray, "The Bringing Church Home Conference" (lecture, Catholic Diocesan Center, Harrisburg, PA, March 16, 2017).

7. Hirsch and Frost, *The Shaping of Things to Come*, 113.

who do the things their master did. He healed people, they healed people; he had dinner with sinners, they sit at tables with sinners; he spent time with the poor, they spend time with the poor. Pastor and author Mark Batterson says that our version of Christlikeness is too civilized. Jesus touched lepers, defended adulterers, befriended prostitutes, washed feet, threw temple tantrums, talked with Samaritans, partied with tax collectors, and regularly offended the Pharirrazzi. Are we following in his footsteps?[8] And are the Jesus Stories enough to create disciples who act and look like the Master? Yes, oh yes. Christ followers who have immersed themselves in Jesus' Stories begin seeping into the cracks and crevices of society with Christlike thinking, Christlike behavior, and a Christlike presence.[9] I dare say that Jesus Stories are the very definition of discipleship. And Jesus Stories are the direct cause of the gritty Christlike disciples Batterson spoke of.

Hebraic versus Greek

The Hebraic world that Jesus inhabited held a different approach to learning than did the Greek world Paul inhabited. This is seen directly in the cultural assumptions of human transformation:

Greek Transformation Theory	Hebraic Transformation Theory
Mind →Emotions →Behavior	Behavior →Emotions →Mind

The Greek model of human change begins by teaching the mind, then assumes new emotions will form around that teaching, which will drive behavioral change. We in the West are completely fa-

---

8. Mark Batterson, *In a Pit with a Lion on a Snowy Day* (Colorado Springs: Multnoman, 2006), 153.

9. Alton Garrison, *Hope in America's Crisis* (Springfield, MO: Gospel Publishing House, 2007), 40.

miliar with this learning approach. However, Jesus derived his transformational patterns from the Hebraic culture, which begins by asking the student to engage a new behavior first and without much explanation, then assumes a new set of emotions will form to continue the behavior, and finally the mind will figure out how to explain the new behavior.

In comparing the two theories, we see an inherent weakness in the Greek pattern, in that many students can learn things in their mind and even feel some new emotions but never really get around to changing their behaviors to match their knowledge. The Hebraic approach doesn't struggle to see behavioral change, because it is demanded up front. Then the emotions and the mental explanations are sure to follow. We see this Hebraic model lived out in Luke 10, when Jesus sent out the disciples to heal, preach, and cast out demons. They came back excited that the same power Jesus had exhibited was flowing from them as well. Notice the learning pattern: he sent them out (behavior), then they came back excited (emotion), and tried to explain their anointing and effectiveness (mind). This was the Hebraic change process at work.

In our Greek-based world, we direct our students into one Bible study after another, but when it comes to taking up the actual works of Christ, these students tend to stall out. They can recite the verses but cannot heal anyone, stare down evil, preach to the poor, or do anything that populates heaven. There is a reason we spend more time in the Epistles than the Gospels. The Epistles are more Greek and are more graspable for us. But the Epistles do not clarify Christlike behaviors like the Jesus Stories do. What is needed for disciple-making is the transformation that flows from deep dives into the life of Christ, which is offered by the Gospel stories. Jesus healed, so we start healing people; Jesus faced down evil, so we do the same; Jesus spent time with the poor, so we start pouring into the lives of the marginalized; Jesus preached in a way that populated heaven, so we start looking for ways to preach to unreached people rather than to rooms full of Christians. Inspire Christlike behavior up front, and the rest of the disciples' formation will follow.

Organic Disciple-Making

Disciple-making is not done on a conveyor belt, though we moderns have tried to make it that way. Making disciples who are capable of replicating the behaviors of Christ is a relational nurturing process. Dan Kimball states that 80 percent of true discipleship and spiritual growth occurs from mentoring, smaller group gatherings, relationships, and serving; only 20 percent is a result of weekend gatherings.[10] J. R. Briggs points out that discipleship is actually a rather messy and inexact process (see diagram).

How we think of Discipleship   How Discipleship actually works

Christlike formation involves ups and downs and learning and unlearning and submission and resistance over and over again. Discipleship systems are not up to such a task, but organic discipleship environments are what is needed.

Contrary to our programmatic approaches, discipleship was not intended to be complex. According to the Gospels, disciple-

---

10.   Kimball, *Emerging Worship*, 29.

ship is merely being with Jesus and being sent out by Jesus.[11] Christian author Thom Rainer adds that Jesus called, built, and sent his disciples. His was a simple discipleship process.[12] The early church embraced simplicity and engaged in obedience-based discipleship that happened on a daily basis in their homes.[13] Organic environments become important for behavioral Christlike formation.

This is where the Jesus Stories and Jesus tables shine. They have a history of turning out disciples like Peter, James, John, Matthew, Luke, Paul, and other power hitters of the Gospel. The closer you get to a dinner table, the closer you get to a natural forum of disciple-making. Conversely, the further you get away from the familial environment, the more difficult disciple-making becomes. We can teach scripture-based discipleship in classrooms quite easily, but if we desire to develop the Christlike behaviors of healing, confronting evil, preaching to the poor, and other repeating works of Christ, we will likely need to employ Jesus Stories at Jesus tables. Traditional Christians often look at dinner churches critically because they do not teach the Bible well. But leaders would disagree with that assessment and proclaim that table environments are able to do the important work of discipleship better than the traditional churches.[14] Leonard Sweet says, "Tables are the place where true discipleship is born."[15] Of course this is true;

---

11. Cray, "The Bringing Church Home Conference." Based on Mark 3:14–15 (NLT): "Jesus appointed twelve of them. . . . They were to accompany him, and he would send them out to preach, giving them authority to cast out demons."

12. Thom Rainer and Eric Geiger, *Simple Church* (Nashville: B&H, 2006), 162.

13. Rob Wegner and Jack Magruder, *Missional Moves: 15 Tectonic Shifts That Transform Churches, Communities, and the World* (Grand Rapids, MI: Zondervan, 2012), 90.

14. Michael Frost, "Bible Teaching Can Happen at the Table Not Just the Pulpit," May 7, 2020, https://mikefrost.net/bible-teaching-can-happen-at-the-table-not-just-the-pulpit/.

15. Sweet, *From Tablet to Table*, 50.

you cannot sit at a Jesus table and not talk about Jesus. And you cannot talk about Jesus for long without enfolding his behaviors into your behaviors. It just happens.

Baptism

Jesus' baptism unfolded dramatically with the form of a dove descending on him as he came out of the water. This was surprising to the onlookers. From a spiritual perspective we can rightly say that the dove followed by the voice from heaven was evidence of both the Holy Spirit and the Father attending the Son's baptism. But there is another interesting perspective to consider. Roman culture had a deep impact on Jewish culture by the time Jesus arrived. In other words, Roman happenings were understood by the Jews. Interestingly, the Roman emperors were chosen based on the augur of an eagle; the leader who had an eagle augur on him, or swoop down over him, would be identified as Jupiter's representative on the earth and Jupiter's choice for emperor. This is where the term *inauguration* originated.[16] So, when the Holy Spirit in the form of a dove augured down on Jesus, it was a take-your-breath-away moment for the people. When the voice from the sky said, "This is my son in whom I am well pleased" (Mark 1:11), that crowd realized that they were experiencing a divine selection event in real time, but this time with Yahweh and his son. Thus, rumors about Jesus being the Messiah started at his baptism (John 1:40–41).

Baptism is a wonderful depiction of discipleship. While I am not one who holds water baptism as necessary for entry into the kingdom of God, I do acknowledge that it is an act of demonstra-

---

16. Streett, *Subversive Meals*, 118–19.

tion that one has decided to follow Jesus. I also recognize that baptism is a metaphor that reveals the discipleship process. In John 3 we find a wonderful interaction between Jesus and a religious leader named Nicodemus. They were discussing that people needed to be born again to enter the kingdom. Nicodemus became altogether too practical with the born-again statement, but Jesus explained that just as an infant is born from a world of water into a world of air, so we go from a world of self to a world of Spirit. In other words, we move from a state of being self-ruled to a state of being Spirit-ruled. This is demonstrated by the imagery of baptism—moving from a world of water where human life cannot be sustained to a world of air where we can breathe and flourish. Baptism and discipleship are umbilically linked. Baptism is a picture of complete and total change, which is the goal of discipleship as well.

Anonymous sources speak of new believers in the early church being brought out of the water with a proclamation being said over them, "Another Jesus, sent to the world!" Forming people to replicate Jesus' words and works was the goal of discipleship for the first church, which was modeled so beautifully in the baptism rite. Though it was lost in antiquity for a time, the "little Jesus" idea is making a recovery. Alan Hirsch talks about "The Little Jesus Conspiracy," which is the divine aim to fill the world with lots of little Jesuses and create an active Christlike redemptive presence in every neighborhood and every sphere of life.[17]

At one of our dinner churches in Seattle I asked one of the guests if I could pray for his healing. He snapped at me angrily, "Why would you ever ask me such a thing?" I told him that this was a Jesus table and that we endeavored to do the things Jesus

---

17. Hirsch, *The Forgotten Ways*, 114.

did, to which he fired back, "Yeah, but you aren't Jesus!" I didn't want to berate this guest and debate the point with him, but all Christ followers walk in the dust of our Jesus and are expected to replicate his works.

For all the metaphors of baptism that have been practiced through the centuries, Paul offered the deepest understanding in Romans 6:3–5(NLT):

> Or have you forgotten that when we were joined with Christ Jesus in baptism, we joined him in his death? For we died and were buried with Christ by baptism. And just as Christ was raised from the dead by a glorious power of the Father, now we also may live new lives. Since we have been unified with him in his death, we will also be raised to life as he was.

This verse gives insight into an understanding of baptism that is far deeper than merely a step in the discipleship process, like many churches practice. For Paul and the first church, being immersed in water was representative of becoming immersed into the life of Jesus. Thus, going into the water was emblematic of dying to their own lives, and being brought out of the water was emblematic of being resurrected so they could live in Jesus' life.

Today, we talk about inviting Jesus into our life far more than we talk about living in Jesus' life. But he wants us to delve into his life too. That immersion is the greater immersion that Paul spoke of further in Philippians 1:5, about having fellowship with the Gospel; in Philippians 2:1, as having fellowship in the Spirit; and in Philippians 3:10, as having fellowship with Jesus' sufferings. The point is this: there is a deep fellowship with the life of Jesus to be experienced by his disciples.

To put it another way, discipleship is becoming immersed into the life, the miracles, the death, the resurrection, the ascension, the mission, and all the stories about Jesus. In Ephesians 5:26, Paul uses baptism language to show what happens when we are immersed into Christ: "it makes us holy and clean, washed by the cleansing of God's word, so we will become a glorious church without spot or wrinkle or any other blemish." Disciples are the result of becoming baptized into the life and times and words and teachings and stories of Jesus.

Necessary for the Kingdom

A large view of church history reveals a primary image for each era: (1) The Apostolic era was laser-focused on the life and stories of Jesus, (2) the Christendom era celebrated the cathedral as its central image, 3) and the Reformation era that we live in has held the Bible as its central image of faith. To prove this, one would only have to dismiss a congregation after worship, offering, and announcements without providing a Bible teaching; the saints would not be happy. Why? Because we are a Bible-centric church. Some go so far to suggest that some Christians are iconic about the Bible to the point of nearing bibliolatry. While I do not fully share that perspective, I do recognize how we have become formed this way.

In the 1500s, the new Protestant gatherings were designed around the classroom sociology complete with lecturers at the front of the room and written materials. The timing could not have been more perfect, because the invention of the Gutenberg Press now made it possible for everyone to have their own copy of the Holy Book, which was something only the priests had access to previously. In these new churches, people were given access to the scriptures for themselves and were told to pay sober attention to the preacher, because they needed to learn how to be the priests of their own salvation. After all, they had walked away from their Catholic priests. This was serious work, and they were lectured from a stage by their pastor about rightly dividing the word of truth. Christian author Tim Dearborn states that it was common for a pastor to set up an hourglass on the podium so the people would get a solid hour of Bible instruction to grow them into their priesthood.[18] In other words, church was an entry-level seminary class. And here we are 500 years later still practicing the same socio-form of Christian gatherings, which continue to be organized around the biblical teaching moment.

This is a different missiological day than sixteenth-century Europe. In that day, Europe was completely Christianized with everyone attending a Catholic church, or perhaps one of the up-rising protest churches if they lived near one.[19] In our day, only 20 percent of the US population attends church. Continuing to focus our discipleship on the study of scriptures, as was appropri-ate when everyone already attended church, needs to be honestly reviewed. As wonderful as it is to study the Holy Book, in these days we don't need more students quoting scripture as much as we need students replicating the salvific behaviors of Jesus. This day demands something punchier. Tim Johnson says that church folk are seldom helpful for the kingdom, and kingdom folk are never welcomed in the church.[20] I think Tim is right. If we keep letting the church folk define what discipleship is, their churches

---

18.   Tim Dearborn and Scott Coil, *Worship at the Next Level* (Grand Rapids MI: Baker 2004), 64.

19.   Jim Heugel, "The Reformation" (lecture to master's class, Northwest Uni-versity, Kirkland, WA, February 15, 2011).

20.   Tim Johnson, "Pastors Pain" (panel discussion, New Room Conference, Murfreesboro, TN, September 23, 2021).

won't be moving mountains any time soon. We need a version of discipleship that disturbs those church folk.

Theology professor Brent Laytham talks about the rush gamblers experience when they have something to lose and says that we need to revisit the place of risk in Christian discipleship, because the wild God of the exodus and the resurrection offers a thrill ride second to none.[21] Throughout history, when secular forces have threatened to sideline the church, it is the emergent discipleship movements that have pointed people back to Christianity's ability to restore lives.[22] Interestingly, the fastest-growing church in the world is the underground church in the Middle East. The Iranian Awakening is a rapidly reproducing discipleship movement that owns no property, has no central leadership, and is predominantly led by women.[23] Awesome. Challenging situations like this clarify the role of discipleship—to ready a rugged people to advance the kingdom of God in scary places. This is who Jesus was.

Delving deeply into Jesus' stories naturally leads us to climb into a life focused on advancing the kingdom of God against all odds. According to Ephesians 2:10, "we are God's handiwork, created in Jesus to do good works, which God prepared in advance for us to do." In other words, we are being crafted by Jesus and his stories to do great works. Tom Sine says that discipleship requires us to set aside our ambitions and join God's conspiracy that focuses on the well-being of others.[24] This, then, is the handiwork

---

21. Brent Laytham, *Ipod, YouTube, Wii Play* (Eugene, OR: Cascade, 2012), 108.

22. Philip Meadows, "Missions and Discipleship in a Digital Culture," *Journal of the International Association for Mission Studies* 29, no. 2 (2012): 177.

23. "What's Happening in Afghanistan?," podcast, *Made for This with Jennie Allen*, April 20, 2021, https://www.jennieallen.com/blog/the-underground-church.

24. Tom Sine, *The New Conspirators* (Downers Grove, IL: InterVarsity, 2008), 124.

of the Jesus' Stories—they inspire disciples to replicate the works of Jesus with power.

Practical Approaches

Making disciples using the *kerygma* is conversational in nature; it is also apprentice based. So start prioritizing the Jesus Stories with your students in readings and discussions. In time, they will become so immersed in the Jesus Stories that the Jesus Works will start pouring out of them.

To give you an outline, liturgical lectionaries are available that contain the Gospels in three-year cycles. The strong point of using lectionaries is that they line up the seasonal stories of the church calendar.

Another outline option is to use the Jesus Stories Bible, available at www.DinnerChurch.Com/Resources. This Bible will take your students through each of the Jesus Stories in the Gospels and Acts in story-form layout. After reading a story, talk about the portions that stand out to them, the questions that emerge, and the behaviors of Christ that are visible. Then look for opportunities to get them busy replicating the works of Jesus they have been reading and discussing.

Build My Church–
by Listening to Me

I love the topic of Christian leadership. My eyes are drawn to anyone who is speaking and writing about it. There is a rather mysterious gospel narrative that offers a loud directive for church leaders to prioritize Jesus' words in their craft of leadership: the transfiguration of Jesus told in Matthew 17. However, this is not a stand-alone story; it actually begins one chapter earlier as Jesus walked with the disciples to Caesarea Philippi. That region was usually considered off limits for any righteous Jew because it was a haven for deep pagan religious practice. It appears that Jesus pointed to the three ornate and awe-inspiring temples that were built against the cliffs and asked his disciples, "Who do people say that I am?" (Matt. 16:13). That question prompted Peter's inspired declaration that he was the Messiah, the Son of the living God. To that Jesus prophesied that his church would be built on the Peter-like declarations about him being the Messiah. And if that weren't enough, he stated that the keys to the kingdom of heaven would be given to the disciples—that whatever they released or bound on earth would be authorized from heaven. In other words, a tremendous amount of spiritual authority has been entrusted to them for giving leadership to the inbreaking kingdom.

Then only six days later Jesus took Peter, James and John up to the mountain of transfiguration. (Matt. 17:1ff) It is there where Jesus took on a glorified appearance and met with Elijah and Moses who had descended to talk with him. This was all so wonderful that Peter was ready to launch into three building programs, because what he had just witnessed was much cooler than the spirituality of the three cliff-side temples he had just seen days earlier. While Peter was still drawing up the architectural plans in his mind, the voice of God thundered down, "This is my son, whom I love; with him I am well pleased. Listen to him!" (Matt. 17:5 NIV)

This is a powerful directive for all Christian leaders to meditate on. God the Father is not very interested in best practices of earthly temples, nor does he seem to be as interested in buildings and programs as we tend to be. What he is interested in is that the leaders of the church spend their most focused attention listening to his son, Jesus the Christ! This divine preference is punctuated by the fact that at no other point in biblical history did a voice thunder down from heaven directing us to listen to Paul, Peter, John, or any other of the thirty-nine authors of the Bible. But it did thunder this one time—that we should listen to Jesus. That should mean something.

In an honest overview, it appears that most staffs, boards, and leadership teams are drawing their proposals from the business world and best practices from other churches. That makes sense given that the church has adopted a social structure that is aligned with other academic and practiced models of human organization that have developed over the past 500 years. However, there are some leaders and authors who push away from business models and instead focus on leadership insights from scripture. I find these approaches to be refreshing because I tire of efforts that reduce the church to align with Ted Talks and best practices. And yet, many of these leaders have instinctively looked to Paul's writings and the pastoral letters for leadership insights. Only in recent decades has there been a move toward christological leadership principles, which is even more refreshing. Out of this recent pursuit have the ideas of servant-leadership and prayer-leadership emerged. These are wonderful growth steps for church leaders.

Question: Do you think Jesus would come to this earth, establish a new kingdom, and then depart without leaving the necessary leadership directions behind for his leaders to continue his mission? How you answer this question determines if you are looking for principles of leadership or actual leadership directions from the stories Jesus told. But this challenges our myopia. We give more authority for leadership to Paul than we give to Jesus. To repeat something I stated earlier, popular evangelical theology comes from the Epistles when it actually needs to come from Gospels.[1] Recovering the centrality of the *kerygma* and the Jesus Stories enables a fresh epistemology to flow into us. The Jesus Stories are not just for entry-level believers; they are also for seasoned leaders who are searching for "the mind of Christ" (1 Cor. 2:16).

We shouldn't be surprised by the idea that the Jesus Stories are for leaders too. After all, almost one-third of all Gospel verses were spoken solely to the disciples, teaching them about leadership in Christ's kingdom. Once our leadership team in Seattle embraced this, we started looking for the mind of Christ in the Jesus Stories. This epistemological change in the cockpit of our church did more to open the future for us than any other transformational material available to the church. Even now, sixteen

---

1. David Olson, presentation at the New Conspirators Conference, Bethany Community Church, Seattle, WA, February 2008.

years into the dinner church chapter, Melodee and I draw all of our pastors and teams together for a weekly leader's dinner. There we meditate on Jesus' stories for timely directives that address our present leadership challenges. In that simple way the mind of Christ is made fresh among us as we pastor a multitude of dinner churches throughout our city. We have discovered that the Gospels are packed full of leadership content.

What follows are several of the Jesus Stories that have directed, formed, and inspired our church in Seattle over the past sixteen years.

The Lost Sheep

Seventeen years ago, our church and leadership team were stuck in the best practices rut. Even though we were working hard to keep up, our church was stalling. In fact, we were declining by urban attrition, which was 14 percent per year. I felt it was time for some radical leadership conversations. So, we dismissed all of our church programs with the exception of the Sunday morning gatherings, and instead convened all of our leadership teams on Tuesday nights to ask the Lord what to do. For the first couple weeks, we just talked about the state of the church. But then the Spirit seemed to enter the room and we found ourselves talking about the parable of the lost sheep. The conversation we thought was going to be strategic became something akin to soul surgery, and the parables became the scalpel. This Jesus Story told of many sheep that were safe in the shepherd's care, but there was one sheep that had wandered into a harrowing place. As we discussed this parable, we began to see a divine priority for our neighbors who were in a difficult place. This story pricked at our pride a bit. We kind of thought we were the place where Jesus would most likely be on Sunday mornings. After all, we had the best Christian download in that part of our city. But in that moment, we realized that Jesus was focused on everyone else in North Seattle, the ones not in church, the ones not paying attention to heaven's voice, the ones not in a safe spiritual place. An appropriate humility and concern came on us as that story surgically sliced at our self-importance.

I look back to that evening with fondness. It was the first time we felt such leadership direction come to us from a parable. But it wouldn't be the last, because we had to break our reliance on business practices and our matrix of leadership ideas that had been cobbled together over dozens of years. After many more surgeries, we would ultimately be brought to a reliance on the *kerygma*. While we still pay attention to business principles, best practices, and principle-based theologies, the Jesus Stories have provided the timeliest leadership directions for us. This lost sheep story was the first to teach us the leadership intent of the Gospel narratives.

The Lost Coin

The Jesus Story of the lost coin came to us at a time when we were questioning our willingness to make the big changes that were needed. We were OK with small changes but lacked the corporate motivation to consider wide-sweeping changes. Further, everything we had done to date was in view of what we thought was good for our church. We hadn't learned to exist for the need of others. Into that malaise this story about the widow and her lost coin began to speak to us. We realized that a lost coin did not mean the same thing to us as it did to a widow in Palestine 2,000 years ago. Having no social structures in place, that widow had to find that coin or she would not eat that night. None of us knew that level of scarcity. Each of us could lose many dollars and would not wonder if we would be able to eat dinner. But this woman's very survival depended on her making the most out of her meager coins.

We had never considered that, like that widow, our church's survival was connected to our ability to find the lost who lived in our city. We were a good church that felt capable to lead to Jesus anyone who might wander into our services or programs. Further, we had classes and baptism processes in place to do right by any seeker; we were not aloof to the evangelistic vocation. However, it could not be said of us that we were as desperate to find the lost as that widow in the story. That night we watched a parable bring us to an important insight: our survival as a church was directly connected to our ability to find the lost. That was a huge surgery, to be sure, and it brought us to a point of desperation—one that aligned with the divine desperation pouring out of heaven. That meeting ended on a sober note.

The Lost Son

The Jesus Story of the lost son visited our leadership core at the exact moment we needed to formalize a transformational shift. Due to the previous Jesus Stories, we were beginning to feel that heaven had a completely different path for us to traverse. And now it was decision time. The parable of the lost son became the "now" moment for our leaders. This is the story of the prodigal son who took his share of the family estate and left to live a life of indulgence and wanton lust. However, this story challenged our long-standing view of God. Here Jesus revealed a rather shocking picture of the Father as being on the proverbial front porch pacing and pensive and longing and straining to see his son returning home. Our church held the common view of a God calmly sitting on his throne, happy in his heaven, and overseeing the affairs of the universe. But when Jesus spoke of God, he pictured an obsessive and concerned and nervous Father. How do we reconcile the two pictures? As we discussed Jesus' image, we acknowledged that if one of our children had run away from home and headed for the underbelly of Seattle and we were left to wonder what they were drinking or shooting into their veins, whether they were indoors or sleeping in a ditch, whether they were in a hospital or even alive, it would thoroughly change us as parents. Suddenly we got it. We, too, would be watching the front door and listening for the phone in hope that it would be our child coming home. That is what happened to our Father. The fall of man changed what it meant for God to be God, for the Father to be the Father, for Dad to be Dad. No wonder Jesus' story pictured him pacing on the porch. Then when the prodigal son did return, the father's worry turned to relief. And he ran to the boy, kissed him, threw a new coat over his wet shoulders, put a family ring back on his finger, and ordered up a feast.

This Jesus Story made perhaps the deepest surgical impact of all. We now understood the mood of heaven. We understood the divine obsession. We understood this day of salvation. We understood Christianity as the greatest rescue project in the history of the world. In total, we realized that the God family was in the rescue business. However, we were in the Bible-teaching business. We were also in the programs-for-all-ages business and the property management business, as we spent half our budget on our

95

building. But it could not be said of us that we were in the rescue business. It was time to make a change.

Ministerial friends of ours had watched our church fade away and then make an about-face to burst forth with surprisingly strong momentum in the most secular city in the United States. So, we started to hear, "What has changed with you guys?" My answer has always been the same: we changed in a single evening. It was after we finished the lost son parable that thirty-five of our leaders stood up, took hold of hands, and prayed a simple prayer: "Lord, we recognize the God family is in the rescue business, but we have not been. We want back into the family biz." Then we quietly picked up our Bibles and went home. It was unemotional, but we knew that heaven had heard us, and we were now on a very different path. Though it would take a few months for that decision to become visible, we were back in the family biz. This Jesus Story transformed our church's identity in an evening.

The Unfruitful Tree

This Jesus Story emerged at a time when we needed to know why we were failing as a church. As noted earlier, we had been declining at a steep pace, and it was now becoming noticeable in our Sunday gatherings; everyone was looking around the room when they would normally be watching all the ministry flowing from off the stage. Into this moment stepped the parable about the unfruitful tree in the garden. The owner noticed that this tree was not bearing fruit and told the gardener to pull it up. The gardener appealed to be given one more year to fertilize it, prune it, and soften the soil around its roots. If after all that the tree still wasn't producing, he promised to pull it out. I still remember the moment our college pastor blurted out to the rest of the leaders in the room, "This tree is our church! We have been fertilized, our roots have been dug around, and now we are being pruned every week. Still, we are not reaching the lost. This tree is us!" Always be careful when the college pastor has something to say. That was a lot of truth being dumped into that leadership room that night. But he was right. This was a perfect picture of us. We further acknowledged that if we did not become effective at bringing our secular neighbors to the faith, Jesus himself would pull our church from his garden. In fact, the tugging on our tree was already happening, in the form of our 14 percent declines in attendance paralleling 13 percent declines in finances. We were feeling the financial pinch of our younger families moving away, our older saints dying, and no one coming to replace them. And while this story was a blunt warning, it was actually very helpful. We now saw the exact reason we were failing: we were completely ineffective at reaching the lost. We also saw the exact reason we would start thriving again, to become effective at rescuing the lost who lived around us.

According to the Hartford Institute for Religious Research, the American church has been closing ninety-six churches per week for many years.[2] Of this I am very sure: the churches that closed this past week undoubtedly felt the presence of Jesus during their last gathering, but I'm equally sure it had been a long while since they had led a single secular sinner to the Savior. And so, true to this parable, Jesus let them close. This Jesus Story is almost too blunt for some to handle, but the clarity it creates is a huge blessing for any leadership team. If this is indeed the day

---

2. Hartford Institute for Religious Research, "Fast Facts about American Religion," https://hirr.Hartsem.edu/research/fastfacts/fast-facts.html.

of salvation, and heaven is in a full-court-press to get all the lost sons and daughters back to the Father's table, then of course Jesus will pull the unfruitful churches to make way for the fruitful ones. After this Jesus Story, we knew exactly what we needed to do. We didn't know how yet, but we now knew what was expected of us. The vision of that dried-up tree spoke to us loudly.

The Wineskin

Our Seattle leadership team now felt the calling to become effective at faith conversations with our secular neighbors. But there was nothing in our history that would make this a natural growth step. It was into that leadership challenge that the Jesus Story about the wineskins surfaced. This parable teaches that no one should put new wine into an old wineskin, because they have already expanded once with the first batch of wine. To expect a wineskin to expand another time would be beyond its ability, especially after it had now hardened with the aging wine it previously contained. This would assuredly lead to a split wineskin and spilled wine. While we had read and taught this parable many times, we saw something very different on this night. Our newly forming kerygmatic eyes coupled with a growing belief that the Gospels held leadership directives, allowed us to see that this parable was talking about earthly limitations and divine plans. To be precise: the wineskin represented our way of doing church, while the wine represented the people Jesus had given us to mature. The wineskin had to do with the many things about the church culture we had formed over the decades: our sanctuary setup, worship sound, teaching style, and fellowship structures. These were all things we had liked into existence over time. As we discussed this story, we sensed Jesus ask us a question: "You are wanting me to give you influence with your secular neighbors. If I send them, are you assuming they will be poured into your wineskin? The Sunday Gathering and programs that you have designed for yourselves?" The implications of this question left the room quiet.

So for the first time, we began to wrestle with whether we'd be willing to do church for people who were different than we are and in a way that they need it, even if we don't like it. Quite frankly, it felt rather offensive to consider that our way of doing church might not be awesome for everyone on the planet. How could something we like this much be so wrong for others? We had always imagined that one day we might plant another church or a multisite location. But we assumed our other churches would look and feel like us and be something we could proudly replicate. Now, this story of wineskin was challenging us at the core of our preferences. After some soul searching, we purposed together that we would be willing to plant a church for a different people, in a different way, and without using all the church stuff we liked. I wish I could report that we were all excited about this resolve and left the room looking for a new church to plant. But no. It was a reluctant willingness. Nonetheless, that Jesus Story started opening our hearts to a new way of doing church. In time, that would become critical ground gained for our leadership team and our congregation.

The Great Banquet

Our church was clearly on a transformation journey, and many assumptions were being challenged in our hearts. We had been brought to imagine doing church in a different way, and we discussed reaching for people who were different than we are, but we did not know what all of this might mean. Author Donald McGavern spoke about the Homogeneous Unity Principle, which was necessary for the church growth movement to gather people with others who were like them.[3] We were faithful disciples of the church growth movement. But now, we were considering something that goes against the social science of church growth. It was into that confusion that the story about the great banquet surfaced. Most do not know that this wasn't actually a parable. It was based on an actual occurrence that had been told and retold in oral tradition and later was included in the Talmud.[4] A real king by the name of Bar Mayaan, in the Mediterranean region, had a son who was getting married. But the elites and the nobles of the realm were mad at the king and refused to come. The king was determined not to let his political problems embarrass his son and the bride-to-be, so he instructed his servants to go out and invite the commoners. After that was done, it was obvious that there would still be room in the great hall, so he sent his servants to invite the laundry workers and peasants. Still there were a few seats remaining, to which he told his servants to go to the hedge-rows and even invite the homeless to come, so the banquet hall would be full.

From this story Jesus opened our eyes to a significant leadership truth: Any church that is empty in any way, be it space or finances or ministry resources, should drop down a step on the socioeconomic ladder and focus their mission on those people. And if there is still ministry capacity, drop down again to reach

3. Griffiths, *Shaking the Sleeping Beauty*, 193.
4. Julian Hills and Graydon Snyder, *Common Life in the Early Church* (Harrisburg, PA: Trinity Press International, 1998), 187.

people in a lower layer. And if there is yet still more room, start embracing the homeless and the marginalized into your Jesus family. Here we were trying to get our ministry momentum back but only assuming the same socioeconomic level that made up our present congregation. However, in Jesus' calculus of ministry, momentum is restored when we reach for people who are very different than we are and even live in a lessor economic stratum. I started researching churches across the country that had lost their momentum and then regained it. To my surprise, I found repeatedly that these churches had altered the missional focus to embrace people in their communities who were more challenged financially than their present congregations. Best practices seldom talk about things like this, but we need to, because there are a multitude of churches that are missing this corner and assuming that one day their sanctuaries will again be full of people who are exactly like them. But this story offers a leadership directive that is quite different. It showed us the true nature of mission, momentum, and regaining traction.

The Farmer and the Weeds

The future that awaited us was one of gathering around the historic Jesus tables with secular people whose values and lifestyles were completely removed from what we were used to. Besides that, we were a part of a denominational group with roots in the holiness movement that held to a strong bounded-set approach to theological management. This meant we felt obligated to patrol the boundaries and challenge everyone to begin their faith journey by repenting of all things in their lifestyle not consistent with scripture. Only after that could they enjoy all aspects of the family of faith. It was to that part of our history that the parable of the farmer and the weeds entered our thought-space. This story reveals a man who planted his field, only to have weeds immediately spring up amid the crops. The farmer knew this was not normal and proclaimed that an enemy had done this. When his farmhands heard this, they headed for the shed to grab the hoes and picks intending to weed the garden. When the farmer saw what they were doing, he curtly told them to stop, because in pulling the weeds they would pull up the good crops too. He then explained that other workers would separate the weeds from the crops at harvest time. They were tasked to simply water and nurture the good seed.

Once again Jesus began speaking an important leadership directive to us. We were not to pull the weeds out of the lives of the people he would send to us, but rather trust those lifestyles and issues to be weeded out later. Well, this was a huge challenge to our holiness history. We had always prided ourselves in not being sell-out Christians. We were the ones who defended the scriptures and purified the faith. We pulled the weeds of everybody. And now, it seemed Jesus was asking us to ignore the weeds. We really wrestled with this issue. Could we be good church leaders and not confront the obvious sins in the lives of people who started coming to our dinner churches?

This story was doing something deep within us. We were being asked to grow from serving as good church-people to becoming good evangelists. If Jesus was going to start giving us rooms full of secular and wayward people at our tables, we needed to become a bit more like him—a friend of sinners. Dan Kimball points out that most churches are perceived as being scary, angry, and judgmental.[5] While we were not cruel, our church did feel a certain obligation to help people get free from the sinful weeds in their lives as soon as possible. We had no idea that these subtle communications were creating a chasm between us and the people Jesus wanted us to reach. This parable provided the moment for us to hear Jesus say, "Stop!" We heard him, and we inched past the fear that we would be soft-selling the gospel. In fact, we realized that we weren't being asked to abandon holiness, because every saint and every sinner is still called into the holiness and wholeness of the Christlike life. But we were being asked to stop forcing lifestyle changes on the lost people Jesus would send us. It was our role to befriend them, embrace them, and talk about the Jesus Stories with them, and to trust him with the rest. And that is exactly what happened. At our dinner church tables we watched Jesus start melting away people's brokenness, day by day, grace by grace, and faith by faith. He promised in this parable that he would take care of the weeds one day. As it turns out, Jesus is really good at his job!

Overlooking the Town

We opened our first dinner church in our own building and were immediately surprised by the people who joined us on these Wednesday nights. They were so thankful to be with us to eat and listen to the Jesus preaching. Very quickly, we realized they were willing to talk about the Jesus Stories around the tables, but they were not interested in coming back on Sundays to our worship gatherings. We had jurisdictional leaders from our denomination

5. Dan Kimball, *They Like Jesus but Not the Church* (Grand Rapids, MI: Zondervan, 2007), 32.

who visited, and they were surprised by the people willing to join us around tables but not return on Sundays. Based on everything church consultants were saying, it made no sense. Soon we felt directed to open up our first off-site dinner church in a neighborhood a couple miles south of our church campus. For many months we had felt called into the Greenwood neighborhood of Seattle by a spiritual stirring that can only be explained as a Macedonian-like encounter. So, when we opened that dinner church, the room started to fill up very quickly, and within six months that banquet room was totally filled with people who were very different than our Sunday gatherings. Then another neighborhood started stirring in our spirits, and the same thing occurred. We did not know why we were gaining such traction right now, especially when Seattleites were so unwilling to join us at our primary campus for years. But momentum was returning.

Into this leadership question we started to see a pattern from numerous Jesus Stories about how he approached new cities. Jesus often stood and overlooked the family farms, villages, towns, and cities before he walked into them. Sometimes he just watched the comings and goings of people, and at other times he was moved to compassion by the needs he saw from those overwatch positions.[6] Then in the early chapters of Mark's Gospel, we see Jesus going from town to town with his disciples, healing by day and eating with sinners by night. It was apparent that Jesus was following a strategy—one that we hadn't studied in seminary. Finally, it came into focus for us as we meditated on Mark 2:16–17: "'Why does your master eat with such scum?' When Jesus heard this, he told them, 'Healthy people don't need a doctor—sick people do. I have

6.   Matthew 9:36; 14:14; 23:37.

not come to call those who think they are righteous, but those who know they are sinners.'"

We heard it. When Jesus was standing up on those overwatch points, he was not only praying over that town but was identifying the gathering points where the broken people were most present. Once Jesus entered a town he would walk by those whose lives were going well, in order to get directly to those whose lives were not going well—the last, the least, the left-behind, and the isolated. His salvific strategy of overlooking the town was so he could see the pockets of pain. This is what was happening to us. The Spirit was drawing us into the same kinds of locations in our city. Now we understood it. Now we could explain it.

It is often said that scripture is contextually observed. In other words, the scripture opens to us based on the needs present in our context. In developed countries, the scriptures seem to say a lot about the love and fulfillment found in Christ. But in poor countries, the scriptures speak to the people about the provision and protection of Jesus. Our church had spent most of its ministry with middle- and upper-class people. Now that we were being drawn into the isolated neighborhoods, the Jesus Stories started opening up possibilities to us in very different ways. Previously, we believed that everyone needed Jesus, and it was our job to serve him up equally wherever we were. Not anymore. Now we saw a picture of Christian leadership that should expect to walk unapologetically right by some circles to be with the desperate, the broken, and those without an advocate. These folks were on a watchlist in heaven, and now we understood that we were to respond to that list as well. Everyone is welcome in Christ's kingdom, but not everyone goes first. Those overlook stories birthed a missiological skill in us and gave us new eyes for discerning our city.

The Day Lightning Fell

The last couple years have not been kind to our city of Seattle. Marches that began at the point of human pain quickly descended into anarchy and criminal takeovers of entire neighborhoods. We have suffered through lengthened shutdowns. City buildings have been burned, and other government buildings have become so crime-ridden that they had to be closed. There has been infighting within our city leaders to the point of mob attacks being led by city officials against other city officials. All of this has culminated with the loss of hundreds of businesses and a downtown that was boarded up and vacant. While some of the business and down-town life is making a slow comeback, the lingering impact has been the overall crime rates. Crime has doubled in almost every category—from murders, to assaults, to break-ins—along with massive visibility of open drug dealing on sidewalks and shoplifting gangs working in unison throughout big box stores, even in daylight hours. These visible criminal activities are not subsiding. We are broken-hearted for our city. Into that grief we were visited by a Jesus Story that surprised us.

In Luke 10 Jesus sent out seventy-two disciples to replicate his works: healing the sick, confronting evil, and preaching the kingdom of heaven. When those disciples returned to Jesus, they were excited and joyfully reported that even the demons ran from them, to which Jesus replied, "Yes, I saw Satan fall from heaven like lightning!" (v. 18). What an interesting picture of the works of Satan's kingdom losing footing, even from the high places. This Jesus Story began to breathe strength into our leadership team at a time when it appeared that evil was engulfing the city we loved. It reminded us that we live in a spiritual war between the uprising kingdom of darkness and the inbreaking kingdom of Jesus. It also reminded us of Jesus' commitment to destroy the works of the devil (1 John 3:8). But mostly, it placed a mantle of Jesus-like authority on our shoulders to confront evil when we saw it. We noted that this was not just the twelve who were given authority over evil. It was the seventy-two. In other words, this was not an insider anointing. It was intended for every disciple of Jesus throughout the ranks of time, including our leadership team in Seattle. However, as the mantle of authority from this story was setting on us, our leaders felt a certain discomfort in their spirits. The imagery of casting out demons seemed difficult to us.

Casting out demons seems to be a repeating refrain in the ministry of Jesus. Of all the works of Christlikeness, it is the one most cumbersome for leaders in the West to comprehend and carry out. Some of this difficulty is that we live in a rational-based part of the world, and thus we struggle with the idea of dealing directly with demons. But there is another issue that clouds our willingness to join Jesus in this aspect of his ministry. I propose there is some theological untangling that is needed. Most leaders are surprised to learn that the idea of demon possession is not listed in the original New Testament. That is a construct from Catholicism for purposes of quantifying the level of demonic harassment. The only terms used in the original text is *demonization* or *demonized*. For example, when a person was being interfered with by an evil presence, it was recorded that they were being *demonized*. This understanding changes things for us in the West. It certainly changed things for our leaders. To stop imagining that we were supposed to exorcise demons and instead grasp the understanding of confronting evil, big or small, aligned with the original New Testament and set more comfortably on our shoulders. Our leaders all acknowledged that there was a wave of evil flooding across our city, and they felt a desire to stand against it in prayer. Now this Jesus Story was adding authority to each of us—an authority that we should expect the uprising kingdom of darkness to lose ground whenever we confront it. James 4:7 used this language: "Resist the devil and he will flee from you." When we see evil affecting people's lives or societal lives, we can put on the authority given to all disciples by Jesus himself to resist evil and destroy the works of the uprising kingdom of darkness. If not us, who?

Last year, I was standing with my wife at Gas Works Park overlooking our city and praying for Jesus to show up and fix it. I sensed something deep in my spirit say, "You fix it! I've placed you in seventeen neighborhoods already, and you understand the power of the historic prayer walk, so *you* start resisting this uprising evil." I was stunned, but I knew it was the voice of the Lord directing our church's next steps. When I shared what happened at Gas Works Park, we started talking about the "fall like lightning" story. We quickly knew that we were to add weekly prayer walks to our dinner church sites. If we were going to resist the uprising evil in our town, we needed to have boots on the ground (i.e., the sidewalks). We determined that we were going to walk the light of Jesus into our neighborhoods in such a way that the uprising darkness would have to retreat. That is what the book says. If we resist evil, that evil will not only retreat but flee. This then is what 2022 meant to Community Dinners in Seattle—putting on the authority Jesus had given and engaging in prayer walks throughout our city, neighborhood by neighborhood and week by week. While we were just getting started, we expected to make a difference in the atmosphere of our sidewalks. We also expected the crime wave to recede, and we expected the quality of life to thrive for our neighbors. This Jesus Story did more than give us a present-day vision of resisting evil. It placed a new anointing on our shoulders.

A Leadership Culture

Our Seattle church has been affected by so many Jesus Stories over the years that we now have a leadership culture that looks for the mind of Christ in the stories of Christ. Recently, our board was facing a weighty financial decision. When I went around the circle asking for each leader's insight, I was amazed by the number of Gospel narratives that emerged. The story that affected us the most that night was a section from Jesus' Sermon on the Mount (Matt. 6:19ff) about not laying up treasures here on earth where moths eat them and rust destroys them, but rather storing our treasures in heaven. In that moment we sensed the Lord directing us in a very clear way, and with a unanimous vote we took a faith step to fund some things that would advance the kingdom even though we could barely afford them. To be steered and confirmed by Jesus Stories has become our new normal.

Practical Approaches

Stepping into kerygmatic leadership is both simple and difficult. It is simple in that it can be employed by asking any church leadership group one question: What story in the Gospels speaks to the situation we are facing or decision we are considering? And it is difficult training your leaders to delve deeply into the life and times and words and stories about Jesus. I assure you that most staff and board members will be able to offer scriptures and verses far more easily than remembering Jesus Stories and contextualizing them into your situation. That then is the leadership challenge. And it only develops by repetition as the leader asks the question, over and over again. And it only reshapes the culture as your team of your team experiences Jesus speaking to them from his gospel material with constancy, over and over again. So start there.

Conclusion

Post-Christian America and the rise of the secular worldview is driving the need for a change in Christian discourse. It would do us well to meditate on Jesus' directives for us to prioritize his words, teachings, and stories.

When Jesus told the story about the wise and foolish builders, he declared that "his words" were the only spiritual materials one could use to build their life on that would withstand all storms. When it comes to our spiritual development, Jesus would say, *Prioritize my words!*

When Jesus hosted the Last Supper, he redirected the focus to "remember him." In so doing, Jesus birthed a New Passover in that first Holy Week. Consequently, the book of Acts reveals the new burgeoning church gathering around tables and talking about Jesus. When it comes to doing church Jesus would say, *Prioritize my life stories!*

When Jesus read from the scroll of Isaiah in the synagogue in Nazareth about his life calling, he declared that his ministry would be focused on breathing favor into the poor, blind, and oppressed. Then after modeling a ministry of healing the sick and preaching to the poor, he sent out his disciples to do same thing. When it comes to pursuing people, Jesus would say, *Offer my favor, and start with the poor, the sick, and the oppressed!*

When Luke recalled the Great Commission, the disciples were to be "witnesses to Jesus"; they were to tell about his life events, teachings, words, and stories. When it comes to evangelism, Jesus would say, *Be witnesses about my life and teachings and stories.*

When Peter remembered the Great Commission, the disciples were to go and preach the gospel stories like Jesus did. When it comes to preaching, Jesus would say, *Go preach the same things you heard me preach!*

When Matthew recollected the Great Commission, they were to make disciples by teaching them what Jesus had taught. When it comes to disciple-making, Jesus would say, *Teach them my words, stories, and life-lessons!*

When Jesus stated that he would build his church on revelations and declarations about the Messiah, and then days later when the audible voice of God thundered down on the transfiguration moment, a deep lesson about leadership was served. When it comes to Christian leadership, Jesus would say, *Build my church by making declarations about me and listening to me!*

Those first disciples took these directives to prioritize Jesus' content seriously. Paul told Timothy never to be ashamed to tell the good-news stories about Jesus (1 Tim. 1:8). And to the Roman Christians he declared that he was not ashamed of the gospel stories, because that is how the power of God poured salvation on the earth (Rom. 1:16). It is interesting to consider how effective the Jesus Stories were at reaching pagan and Gentile populations, and how the church grew from a movement of hundreds to a movement of tens of millions while they were telling and retelling the Jesus Stories around Jesus tables.

There is an outcry today for the simple Gospel stories again. Some years ago Melodee and I attended a conference in which the worship leader's band was grounded because of bad weather. So, the worship leader led the entire conference from a keyboard in the simplest of ways. I doubt she led more than three songs throughout the entirety of the conference, just did the same ones slowly over and over again. You might have thought it would become boring, but no. It was an incredibly powerful time. Simplicity can be a very potent thing.

The Jesus Stories are simple, but whenever they have been prioritized throughout history, the church has gained significant influence. The 468 gospel stories from the life of Christ are the centerpiece and the highpoint of the scriptures. Once we win back the supremacy of the Gospel stories, Apostolic-era results are again possible. As Leonard Sweet says, the ones with the best stories win![7] And that would be us.

---

7.   Sweet, *From Tablet to Table*, 34.

What the First Church Proclaimed

W hat follows are ninety-four scriptural sections from Acts through the end of the New Testament revealing a direct indication that the speaking content of the first church was from the life and stories of Jesus. This was accomplished by searching the following key words: *Preach, Teach, Proclaim,* and *Testify.* Second, in evaluating the context of those searches, ninety-four of the verses identified the subject of their proclamations as being *Jesus, Jesus Christ, the Messiah, the gospel of Jesus, Jesus' Name, our Lord, the Word of the Lord, the Living Word, the kingdom* (an abbreviation that assumed the life work of Jesus), *the Gospel* (an abbreviation that assumed the life of Jesus), and *the Word* (an abbreviation assuming the son of God). Finally, only ten verses using the key words listed above were not clearly stated as Jesus being the subject of their preaching. They, too, are included below. *Note:* all these New Testament searches were done in the New International Version.

Initially, the meaning of this exercise reveals that the big message of the New Testament is they proclaimed Jesus and the Jesus Stories at every turn. Second, this exercise provides the subject and content of the first preachers' communications in their own words. Third, this exercise gives present-day leaders an opportunity to meditate on the difference between "Bible teaching" and "Jesus Stories preaching," which is an important consideration in this day when we are outnumbered by secular people—the New Gentiles.

Acts 2:14ff—Then Peter stood up with the eleven and addressed the crowd. Jesus of Nazareth was accredited with miracles, wonders and signs, was nailed to a cross, but God raised him from the dead, was both Lord and Messiah. Repent and be baptized in the name of Jesus.

Acts 4:2—Proclaiming Jesus and the resurrection.

Acts 5:42—Never stopped proclaiming Jesus as Messiah.

Acts 8:4—Those who had been scattered preached the word wherever they went.

Acts 8:5—Philip proclaimed the Messiah.

Acts 8:12—They believed Philip as he proclaimed the good news and the name of Jesus Christ.

Acts 8:25—After they had proclaimed the word of the Lord and testified about Jesus . . .

Acts 8:40—Philip, however, appeared at Azotus and preached the gospel in all the towns until he reached Caesarea.

Acts 9:15—Paul, a chosen instrument to proclaim Jesus' name.

Acts 9:20—At once he began to preach in the synagogues that Jesus was the Son of God.

Acts 9:27—He preached fearlessly in the name of Jesus.

Acts 10:42—He commanded us to preach and testify that he is the one whom God appointed judge of the living and the dead.

Acts 13:5—They proclaimed the Word of God in synagogues.

Acts 13:38—Jesus, the forgiveness of sins, we proclaimed to you.

Acts 14:21—They preached the gospel in Antioch and won a large number of disciples.

Acts 14:25—When they preached the Word in Perga, they went on to Attalia.

Acts 15:35—Paul and Barnabas remained in Antioch, where they and many others taught and preached the Word of the Lord.

Acts 15:36—Let us go back in all the towns where we first preached the word of the Lord.

Acts 16:6—Paul, having been kept by the Holy Spirit from preaching the word in Asia.

Acts 16:10—After Paul had seen the vision, they concluded God had called them to preach the gospel in Macedonia.

Acts 17:3—We proclaimed why Jesus must suffer, rise from the dead, and is the Messiah.

Acts 17:13—Paul was preaching the Word of God at Berea.

Acts 17:18—Epicureans and Stoic philosophers came to debate Paul as he was preaching the good news about Jesus and the resurrection.

Acts 17:23ff—People of Athens, I proclaim to you . . . the one raised from the dead.

Acts 18:5—Paul devoted himself exclusively to preach and testify Jesus as the Messiah.

Acts 18:24—Apollos spoke with great fervor and taught about Jesus.

Acts 18:28—He vigorously refuted Jewish opponents in public debate that Jesus was the Messiah.

Acts 19:8—Paul entered the synagogue and spoke boldly there for three months, arguing persuasively about the kingdom of God.

Acts 19:13—The sons of sceva . . . in the Name of Jesus whom Paul preaches.

Acts 20:20—I have not hesitated to teach and preach repentance and have faith in our Lord Jesus.

Acts 20:25ff—I have preached the kingdom and proclaimed the whole will of God to you.

Acts 26:20ff—To the Gentiles I preached that they should repent and turn to God, and that the Messiah would suffer and rise from the dead and bring light to his people and the Gentiles.

Acts 28:31—Paul proclaimed the kingdom and taught about the Lord Jesus Christ with all boldness.

Rom. 1:9—I serve by preaching the gospel of God's Son.

Rom. 1:15ff—I am so eager to preach the gospel in Rome, for I am not ashamed of the gospel; it is the power of God that brings salvation to anyone who believes—Jew and Gentile.

Rom. 10:8ff—The message of faith we proclaim: declare Jesus as Lord and you'll be saved.

Rom. 10:14—How can they call on the Lord Jesus Christ without someone preaching to them?

Rom. 15:16—I am a minister of Jesus Christ proclaiming the gospel to the Gentiles.

Rom. 15:18ff—I will not venture to speak anything except what Christ accomplished through me; I have fully proclaimed the gospel of Christ.

Rom. 15:20—It has always been my ambition to preach the gospel where it is not known, not building on someone else's foundation

Rom. 16:25—The message I proclaim about Jesus Christ in keeping with the mystery hidden for long ages, made known through the prophets, but now available to the Gentiles.

1 Cor. 1:17—Christ sent me to preach the gospel.

1 Cor. 1:23—We preach Christ crucified.

1 Cor. 2:1ff—I came proclaiming the testimony about God, resolving to know nothing but Jesus Christ; my message and preaching were not with wise and persuasive words.

1 Cor. 9:14—Those who preach the gospel should receive their living from the gospel.

1 Cor. 9:16—When I preach the gospel, I am compelled to preach. Woe to me if I don't preach the gospel.

1 Cor. 9:18—In preaching the gospel, I offer it free of charge.

1 Cor. 9:27—After I have preached (for the sake of the gospel) I myself won't be disqualified for the prize.

1 Cor. 11:26—When you eat this bread you proclaim the Lord's death until he comes.

1 Cor. 15:1ff—The gospel I preached . . . Jesus died for your sins.

1 Cor. 15:12—We preached that Christ has been raised from the dead.

1 Cor. 15:14—If Christ has not been raised our preaching is useless and so is your faith.

2 Cor. 1:19—Jesus Christ who was preached among you.

2 Cor. 2:12—Preached the gospel of Christ in Troas.

2 Cor. 4:5—What we preach is not of ourselves, but Jesus Christ.

2 Cor. 10:15ff—Our hope is that your faith grows, so that we can preach the gospel in the regions beyond you.

2 Cor. 11:4—If anyone comes preaching any Jesus other than the Jesus we preached . . .

2 Cor. 11:7—Was it a sin for me to lower myself in order to elevate you by preaching the gospel?

Gal. 1:8—Even if we heard from an angel to preach a different gospel than the one we preached to you, let them be under God's curse.

Gal. 1:9—I say it again, if anybody is preaching to you a gospel other than what you accepted, let them be under God's curse.

Gal. 1:11—The Gospel I preached was not of human origin, I received it by revelation from Jesus Christ.

Gal. 1:16—To reveal his son in me so that I might preach him among the Gentiles.

Gal. 1:23—The man who formerly persecuted us is now preaching the faith.

Gal. 2:2—I presented the gospel that I preach among the Gentiles.

Gal. 2:7—They recognized I had been entrusted with the task of preaching the gospel to the uncircumcised.

Gal. 4:13—It was because of an illness that I first preached the gospel to you.

Gal. 5:11—If I am still preaching circumcision, the cross has been abolished.

Eph. 2:17—He came and preached peace to you who were far and near.

Eph. 3:8—I preach to the Gentiles the boundless riches of Christ.

Eph. 4:21—When you heard about Christ and were taught in accordance with the truth in Jesus.

Phil. 1:14—Boldly proclaim the gospel without fear; some preach Christ out of rivalry and others preach Christ out of goodwill. Either way Christ is being preached.

Phil. 1:17—The former preach Christ out of envy, supposing they can stir up trouble.

Phil. 1:18—But what does it matter? Whether false motives or true, Christ is preached.

Col. 1:23—This gospel that has been proclaimed to the whole earth, of which I have become its servant.

Col. 4:3–4—Pray for an open door that we may proclaim the mystery of Christ, and that I will proclaim clearly

1 Thess. 2:9—We worked night and day in order not to be a burden to anyone while we preached the gospel of God to you.

2 Thess. 2:14—Called to you through our gospel to share in the glory of Jesus Christ.

1 Tim. 3:16—The mystery: he appeared in the flesh, was preached among the nations, was believed in the world, was taken up in glory.

1 Tim. 4:10–13—The Savior of all people, command and teach and preach these things, and devote yourself to the public reading of scripture.

1 Tim. 5:17—Elders who direct the affairs of the church are worthy of double honor, especially those who teach and preach.

2 Tim. 4:2—Preach the word; be prepared in season and out.

2 Tim. 4:17—But the Lord stood at my side and gave me strength, so that through me the message might be fully proclaimed to the Gentiles.

Titus 1—Jesus Christ, this appointed season brought to light through preaching.

1 Pet. 1:11ff—Sufferings of the Messiah and the glories to follow were spoken to you by those who preached the gospel.

1 Pet. 1:25—The word of the Lord endures forever, and this is the word that was preached to you.

1 Pet. 4:6—For this reason the gospel was preached even to the dead . . .

Heb. 4:2—We have had the good news proclaimed to us.

Heb. 4:6—These who formerly had the good news proclaimed to them.

1 John 1:1—We proclaim the Word of Life, which we have seen with our own eyes.

1 John 1:2—The life appeared; we have seen it and testify to it and proclaim to you eternal life.

1 John 1:3—We proclaim what we have seen, so you may have fellowship with us as we have fellowship with the Father and his Son, Jesus Christ.

The 10 verses that do not identify Jesus as the subject:

Acts 10:37—The baptism John preached . . .

Acts 13:24—Before the coming of Jesus, John preached repentance and baptism.

Acts 15:21—The law of Moses had been preached in every city from the earliest times.

Rom. 2:21—You who teach others do not teach yourself. You who preach against stealing, do you steal?

Rom. 9:17—I raised up Pharaoh that I might display my power and my name be proclaimed.

2 Thess. 2:4—The man of lawlessness—proclaiming himself to be God.

2 Pet. 2:5—He protected Noah, a preacher of righteousness.

Heb. 9:19—When Moses had proclaimed every command of the law . . .

Rev. 5:2—A mighty angel proclaiming, "Who is worthy to open . . ."

Rev. 14:6—I saw another angel flying. He had the eternal gospel to proclaim to those on earth.

A Guide to Telling Jesus Stories

T he stories about Jesus—and the stories Jesus told—have changed the world. They are still changing it today. Here are three steps to help you learn to tell these powerful stories to others. Use this guide alone or, better yet, with a small group of friends.

STEP 1: *Let the story get inside you!*

- Choose a story.
- Start with a shorter story, such as:
  - ▶ "A Storm" as told by Mark (found in *Jesus Stories*, page 85)
  - ▶ "A Dying Girl and a Sick Woman" as told by Matthew (found in *Jesus Stories* page 19)
- Later, try a longer one, such as:
  - ▶ "An Official who Refused to Forgive" as told by Matthew (found in *Jesus Stories*, pages 43-44)
- Read the story a few times silently and aloud.
- Ask others to read the story to you. Listen to them as they read it.
- Once you've read and heard the story a few times, ask and discuss the following questions:
  - ▶ What do I like about this story?
  - ▶ What bothers me about this story?
  - ▶ What does it say about God?
  - ▶ What does it say about me and other people?
  - ▶ What is one thing I can do to make this part of my life?
  - ▶ What will I do with this story? Share it? Apply it? Spend more time with it?

 AMERICAN BIBLE SOCIETY

STEP 2: *Let the story affect you!*

Ask and discuss these questions to help you notice how the story of Jesus is affecting you:

- ► How does the story make me feel?
- ► Is there conflict?
- ► Who is Jesus talking to?
- ► Are there any characters I identify with?
- ► Are there details that have particular meaning for me? for my community? for the world?
- ► What parts don't I understand?
- ► Does this story make me want to change?
- ► Does this story make me think of someone to share it with?

STEP 3: *Let the story flow out of you!*

- Practice telling your Jesus story to someone else.
- Be yourself! There's no need to be dramatic when you tell the story.
- Use these questions to learn to tell the story naturally without memorizing it:
  - ► What aspect of the story do I want to highlight?
  - ► What details help make that point?
  - ► What details seem confusing or less helpful?
  - ► How do I introduce the story to different people in different contexts— dinner tables, casual conversations, different events?
  - ► Have I put the story in words that are understandable, accurate, and interesting?
  - ► How will I help my listener want to tell the story to someone else?
- After you tell your story, describe the experience to a friend or small group. What happened?
- If possible, invite new listeners to go through the questions in Steps 1 and 2. What new perspectives do they bring?

Closing Invitation

Pray that the stories of Jesus become second nature to you and to all who hear them from you. May Jesus Stories become part of your everyday lives, shaping you, and flowing naturally out of you to others.

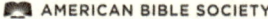 AMERICAN BIBLE SOCIETY   2021-07

468 Stories from the Life of Christ

ACCORDING TO MATTHEW
(152 Stories)

CHAPTER 1

The Ancestors of Jesus
The Birth of Jesus

CHAPTER 2

Wise Men
The Escape to Egypt
The Killing of the Children
The Return from Egypt

CHAPTER 3

The Preaching of John the
  Baptist
The Baptism of Jesus

CHAPTER 4

Jesus and the Devil
Jesus Begins His Work
Jesus Chooses Four
  Fishermen
Jesus Teaches, Preaches,
  and Heals

CHAPTER 5

The Sermon on the Mount
Blessings
Salt and Light
The Law of Moses
Anger
Marriage
Divorce
Promises
Revenge
Love

CHAPTER 6

Giving
Prayer
Worshiping God by Going
  without Eating
Treasures in Heaven
Light
Money
Worry

CHAPTER 7

Judging Others
Ask, Search, Knock
The Narrow Gate
A Tree and Its Fruit
A Warning
Two Builders

CHAPTER 8

Jesus Heals a Man
Jesus Heals an Army
  Officer's Servant
Jesus Heals Many People
Some Who Wanted to Go
  with Jesus
A Storm
Two Men with Demons in
  Them

CHAPTER 9

Jesus Heals a Crippled Man
Jesus Chooses Matthew
People Ask about Going
  without Eating
A Dying Girl and a Sick
  Woman
Jesus Heals Two Blind Men
Jesus Heals a Man Who
  Could Not Talk
Jesus Has Pity on People

CHAPTER 10

Jesus Chooses His Twelve
  Apostles
Instructions for the Twelve
  Apostles
Warning about Trouble
The One to Fear
Telling Others about Christ

Not Peace, but Trouble
Rewards

CHAPTER 11

John the Baptist
The Unbelieving Towns
Come to Me and Rest

CHAPTER 12

A Question about the
  Sabbath
A Man with a Crippled
  Hand
God's Chosen Servant
Jesus and the Ruler of the
  Demons
A Tree and Its Fruit
A Sign from Heaven
Return of an Evil Spirit
Jesus's Mother and
  Brothers

CHAPTER 13

A Story about a Farmer
Why Jesus Used Stories
Jesus Explains the Story
  about the Farmer
Weeds among the Wheat
Stories about a Mustard
  Seed and Yeast
The Reason for Teaching
  with Stories
Jesus Explains the Story
  about the Weeds
A Hidden Treasure
A Valuable Pearl
A Fish Net
New and Old Treasures

The People of Nazareth
Turn against Jesus

CHAPTER 14
The Death of John the
Baptist
Jesus Feeds Five Thousand
Jesus Walks on the Water
Jesus Heals Sick People in
Gennesaret

CHAPTER 15
The Teaching of the
Ancestors
What Really Makes People
Unclean
A Woman's Faith
Jesus Heals Many People
Jesus Feeds Four Thousand

CHAPTER 16
A Demand for a Sign from
Heaven
The Yeast of the Pharisees
and Sadducees
Who Is Jesus?
Jesus Speaks about His
Suffering and Death

CHAPTER 17
The True Glory of Jesus
Jesus Heals a Boy
Jesus Again Speaks about
His Death
Paying the Temple Tax

CHAPTER 18
Who Is the Greatest?
Temptations to Sin

The Lost Sheep
When Someone Sins
Allowing and Not
Allowing
An Official Who Refused
to Forgive

CHAPTER 19
Teaching about Divorce
Jesus Blesses Little
Children
A Rich Young Man

CHAPTER 20
Workers in a Vineyard
Jesus Again Tells about His
Death
A Mother's Request
Jesus Heals Two Blind Men

CHAPTER 21
Jesus Enters Jerusalem
Jesus in the Temple
Jesus Puts a Curse on a Fig
Tree
A Question about Jesus'
Authority
A Story about Two Sons
Renters of a Vineyard

CHAPTER 22
The Great Banquet
Paying Taxes
Life in the Future World
The Most Important
Commandment
About David's Son

CHAPTER 23

Jesus Condemns the
Pharisees and the Teachers
of the Law of Moses
Jesus Loves Jerusalem

CHAPTER 24

The Temple Will Be
Destroyed
Warning about Trouble
The Horrible Thing
When the Son of Man
Appears
A Lesson from a Fig Tree
No One Knows the Day or
Time
Faithful and Unfaithful
Servants

CHAPTER 25

A Story about Ten Girls
A Story about Three
Servants
The Final Judgment

CHAPTER 26

The Plot to Kill Jesus

At Bethany
Judas and the Chief Priests
Jesus Eats the Passover
Meal with His Disciples
The Lord's Supper
Peter's Promise
Jesus Prays
Jesus Is Arrested
Jesus Is Questioned by the
Council
Peter Says He Doesn't
Know Jesus

CHAPTER 27

Jesus Is Taken to Pilate
Pilate Questions Jesus
Death of Judas
Pilate Questions Jesus
Soldiers Make Fun of Jesus
Jesus Is Nailed to a Cross
The Death of Jesus
Jesus Is Buried

CHAPTER 28

Jesus Is Alive
Report of the Guard
What Jesus' Followers
Must Do

ACCORDING TO MARK
(93 Stories)

CHAPTER 1

The Preaching of John the
Baptist
The Baptism of Jesus
Jesus and Satan

Jesus Begins His Work
Jesus Chooses Four
Fishermen
A Man with an Evil Spirit
Jesus Heals Many People
Jesus Heals a Man

CHAPTER 2

Jesus Heals a Crippled
Man
Jesus Chooses Levi
People Ask about Going
without Eating
A Question about the
sabbath

CHAPTER 3

A Man with a Crippled
Hand
Large Crowds Come to
Jesus
Jesus Chooses His Twelve
Apostles
Jesus and the Ruler of
Demons
Jesus' Mother and Brothers

CHAPTER 4

A Story about a Farmer
Why Jesus Used Stories
Jesus Explains the Story
about the Farmer
Light
Another Story about Seeds
A Mustard Seed
The Reason for Teaching
with Stories

CHAPTER 5

A Man with Evil Spirits
A Dying Girl and a Sick
Woman

CHAPTER 6

The People of Nazareth
Turn Against Jesus

Instructions for the Twelve
Apostles
The Death of John the
Baptist
Jesus Feeds Five Thousand
Jesus Walks on the Water
Jesus Heals Sick People in
Gennesaret

CHAPTER 7

The Teaching of the
Ancestors
What Really Makes People
Unclean
A Woman's Faith
Jesus Heals a Man Who
Was Deaf and Could
Hardly Talk

CHAPTER 8

Jesus Feeds Four Thousand
A Sign from Heaven
The Yeast of the Pharisees
and of Herod
Jesus Heals a Blind Man at
Bethsaida
Who Is Jesus?
Jesus Speaks about His
Suffering and Death

CHAPTER 9

The True Glory of Jesus
Jesus Heals a Boy
Jesus again Speaks about
His Death
Who Is the Greatest?
For or against Jesus
Temptations to Sin

CHAPTER 10

Teaching about Divorce
Jesus Blesses Little
  Children
A Rich Man
Jesus again Tells about His
  Death
The Request of James and
  John
Jesus Heals Blind
  Bartimaeus

CHAPTER 11

Jesus Enters Jerusalem
Jesus Puts a Curse on a Fig
  Tree
Jesus in the Temple
A Lesson from the Fig Tree
A Question about Jesus'
  Authority

CHAPTER 12

Renters of a Vineyard
Paying Taxes
Life in the Future World
The Most Important
  Commandment
About David's Son
Jesus Condemns the
  Pharisees and the Teachers
  of the Law of Moses
A Widow's Offering

CHAPTER 13

The Temple Will Be
  Destroyed
Warning about Trouble
The Horrible Thing

When the Son of Man
  Appears
A Lesson from a Fig Tree
No One Knows the Day or
  Time

CHAPTER 14

A Plot to Kill Jesus
At Bethany
Judas and the Chief Priests
Jesus Eats with His
  Disciples
The Lord's Supper
Peter's Promise
Jesus Prays
Jesus Is Arrested
Jesus Is Questioned by the
  Council
Peter Says He Doesn't
  Know Jesus

CHAPTER 15

Pilate Questions Jesus
The Death Sentence
Soldiers Make Fun of Jesus
Jesus Is Nailed to a Cross
The Death of Jesus
Jesus Is Buried

CHAPTER 16

Jesus Is Alive
Jesus Appears to Mary
  Magdalene
Jesus Appears to Two
  Disciples
What Jesus' Followers
  Must Do
Jesus Returns to Heaven

ACCORDING TO LUKE
(145 Stories)

CHAPTER 1

An Angel Tells about the
  Birth of Jesus
The Angel Gabriel Visits
  Mary
Mary Visits Elizabeth
Mary's Song of Praise
The Birth of John the
  Baptist
Zechariah Praises the Lord

CHAPTER 2

The Birth of Jesus
The Shepherds
Simeon Praises the Lord
Anna Speaks about the
  Child Jesus
The Return to Nazareth
The Boy Jesus in the Temple

CHAPTER 3

The Preaching of John the
  Baptist
The Baptism of Jesus
The Ancestors of Jesus

CHAPTER 4

Jesus and the Devil
Jesus Begins His Work
The People of Nazareth
  Turn against Jesus
A Man with an Evil Spirit
Jesus Heals Many People

CHAPTER 5

Jesus Chooses His First
  Disciples
Jesus Heals a Man
Jesus Heals a Crippled
  Man
Jesus Chooses Levi
People Ask about Going
  without Eating

CHAPTER 6

A Question about the
  Sabbath
A Man with a Crippled
  Hand
Jesus Chooses His Twelve
  Apostles
Jesus Teaches, Preaches,
  and Heals
Blessings and Troubles
Love for Enemies
Judging Others
A Tree and Its Fruit
Two Builders

CHAPTER 7

Jesus Heals an Army
  Officer's Servant
A Widow's Son
John the Baptist
Simon the Pharisee

131

CHAPTER 8

Women Who Helped Jesus
A Story about a Farmer
Why Jesus Used Stories
Jesus Explains the Story
    about a Farmer
Light
Jesus' Mother and Brothers
A Storm
A Man with Demons in
    Him
A Dying Girl and a Sick
    Woman

CHAPTER 9

Instructions for the Twelve
    Apostles
Herod Is Worried
Jesus Feeds Five Thousand
Who Is Jesus?
Jesus Speaks about His
    Suffering and Death
The True Glory of Jesus
Jesus again Speaks about
    His Death
Jesus Heals a Boy
Who Is the Greatest?
For or against Jesus
A Samaritan Village
    Refuses to Receive Jesus
Three People Who Wanted
    to Be Followers

CHAPTER 10

The Work of the Seventy-
    Two Followers
The Unbelieving Towns
The Return of the Seventy-
    Two

Jesus Thanks His Father
The Good Samaritan
Martha and Mary

CHAPTER 11

Prayer
Jesus and the Ruler of
    Demons
Return of an Evil Spirit
Being Really Blessed
A Sign from God
Light
Jesus Condemns the
    Pharisees and Teachers of
    the Law of Moses

CHAPTER 12

Warnings
The One to Fear
Telling Others about
    Christ
A Rich Fool
Worry
Treasures in Heaven
Faithful and Unfaithful
    Servants
Not Peace, but Trouble
Knowing What to Do

CHAPTER 13

Turn Back to God
A Story about a Fig Tree
Healing a Woman on the
    Sabbath
A Mustard Seed and Yeast
The Narrow Door
Jesus and Herod
Jesus Loves Jerusalem

CHAPTER 14

Jesus Heals a Sick Man
How to Be a Guest
The Great Banquet
Being a Disciple
Salt and Light

CHAPTER 15

One Sheep
One Coin
Two Sons

CHAPTER 16

A Dishonest Manager
Some Sayings of Jesus
Lazarus and the Rich Man

CHAPTER 17

Faith and Service
Ten Men with Leprosy
God's Kingdom

CHAPTER 18

A Widow and a Judge
A Pharisee and a Tax
  Collector
Jesus Blesses Little
  Children
A Rich and Important Man
Jesus Again Tells about His
  Death
Jesus Heals a Blind Beggar

CHAPTER 19

Zacchaeus
A Story about Ten Servants
Jesus Enters Jerusalem
Jesus in the Temple

CHAPTER 20

A Question about Jesus'
  Authority
Renters of a Vineyard
Paying Taxes
Life in the Future World
About David's Son
Jesus and the Teachers of
  the Law of Moses

CHAPTER 21

A Widow's Offering
The Temple Will Be
  Destroyed
Warning about Trouble
Jerusalem Will Be
  Destroyed
When the Son of Man
  Appears
A Lesson from a Fig Tree
A Warning

CHAPTER 22

A Plot to Kill Jesus
Jesus Eats with His
  Disciples
The Lord's Supper
An Argument about
  Greatness
Jesus' Disciples Will Be
  Tested
Moneybags, Traveling
  Bags, and Swords
Jesus Prays
Jesus Is Arrested
Peter Says He Doesn't
  Know Jesus
Jesus Is Questioned by the
  Council

CHAPTER 23

Pilate Questions Jesus
Jesus Is Brought before
    Herod
The Death Sentence
Jesus Is Nailed to a Cross
The Death of Jesus
Jesus Is Buried

CHAPTER 24

Jesus Is Alive
Jesus Appears to Two
    Disciples
What Jesus' Followers
    Must Do
Jesus Returns to Heaven

ACCORDING TO JOHN
(78 Stories)

CHAPTER 1

The Word of Life
John the Baptist Tells
    about Jesus
The Lamb of God
The First Disciples of Jesus
Jesus Chooses Philip and
    Nathanael

CHAPTER 2

Jesus at a Wedding in Cana
Jesus in the Temple
Jesus Knows What People
    Are Like

CHAPTER 3

Jesus and Nicodemus
Jesus and John the Baptist
The One Who Comes
    from Heaven

CHAPTER 4

Jesus and the Samaritan
    Woman
Jesus Heals an Official's Son

CHAPTER 5

Jesus Heals a Sick Man
The Son's Authority
Witnesses to Jesus

CHAPTER 6

Feeding Five Thousand
Jesus Walks on the Water
The Bread That Gives Life
The Words of Eternal Life

CHAPTER 7

Jesus' Brothers Don't Have
    Faith in Him
Jesus at the Festival of
    Shelters
Officers Sent to Arrest Jesus
Streams of Life-Giving
    Water
The People Take Sides
The Leaders Refuse to
    Have Faith in Jesus

CHAPTER 8

A Woman Caught in Sin

Jesus Is the Light for the
World
You Cannot Go Where I
Am Going
The Truth Will Set You Free
Your Father Is the Devil
Jesus and Abraham

CHAPTER 9

Jesus Heals a Man Born
Blind
The Pharisees Try to Find
Out What Happened

CHAPTER 10

A Story about Sheep
Jesus Is the Good Shepherd
Jesus Is Rejected

CHAPTER 11

The Death of Lazarus
Jesus Brings Lazarus to Life
The Plot to Kill Jesus

CHAPTER 12

At Bethany
A Plot to Kill Lazarus
Jesus Enters Jerusalem
Some Greeks Want to Meet
Jesus
The Son of Man Must Be
Lifted Up
The People Refuse to Have
Faith in Jesus
Jesus Came to Save the
World

CHAPTER 13

Jesus Washes the Feet of
His Disciples

Jesus Tells What Will
Happen to Him
The New Command
Peter's Promise

CHAPTER 14

Jesus Is the Way to the
Father
The Holy Spirit Is
Promised

CHAPTER 15

Jesus Is the True Vine
The World's Hatred

CHAPTER 16

The Work of the Holy
Spirit
Sorrow Will Turn into Joy

CHAPTER 17

Jesus Prays

CHAPTER 18

Jesus Is Betrayed and
Arrested
Jesus Is Brought to Annas
Peter Says He Doesn't
Know Jesus
Jesus Is Questioned by the
High Priest
Peter again Denies that He
Knows Jesus
Jesus Is Tried by Pilate
Barabbas Selected by the
Crowd

CHAPTER 19

Jesus Whipped, Cross-Examined, and Sentenced to Death
Jesus Is Nailed to a Cross
The Death of Jesus
A Spear Is Stuck in Jesus' Side
Jesus Is Buried

CHAPTER 20

Jesus Is Alive
Jesus Appears to Mary Magdalene

Jesus Appears to His Disciples
Jesus and Thomas
Why John Wrote His Book

CHAPTER 21

Jesus Appears to Seven Disciples
Jesus and Peter
Jesus and His Favorite Disciple

SCAN HERE to learn more about Invite Press, a premier publishing imprint created to invite people to a deeper faith and living relationship with Jesus Christ.